How to Make Your Houseplants Love You

How to Make Your Houseplants Love You

Joe Bagley

First published in Great Britain in 2025
by Mitchell Beazley, an imprint of Octopus
Publishing Group Ltd, Carmelite House,
50 Victoria Embankment, London EC4Y 0DZ
www.octopusbooks.co.uk
www.octopusbooksusa.com

An Hachette UK Company
www.hachette.co.uk
The authorized representative in the EEA is Hachette Ireland,
8 Castlecourt Centre, Dublin 15, D15 XTP3, Ireland
(email: info@hbgi.ie)

ISBN: 9781784729684

A CIP record of this book is available from the British Library

Set in Mamut/Cantoria

Printed and bound in China

Conceived, designed and produced by
The Bright Press, an imprint of the Quarto Group,
1 Triptych Place, London SE1 9SH

www.quarto.com

Publisher	James Evans
Editorial Director	Isheeta Mustafi
Art Director	Emily Nazer
Editor	Nick Pierce
Project Editor	Julie Brooke, Dominique Page
Designer	Josse Pickard
Copyeditor	Katie Crous
Publishing Assistant	Jemima Solley
Picture research	Katie Greenwood
Illustrations	Sarah Skeate
Photographer	Andrew Perris
Consultant	Dr Ross Bayton

Publisher for Mitchell Beazley: Alison Starling

Assistant Editor for Mitchell Beazley: Ellen Sleath

Bright Press wish to thank Suzanne Barnes and Goldcliff's Garden
Centre for their assistance.

Front cover: Shutterstock/Tanya Sid.

Back cover: Shutterstock/Chansom Pantip (top);
Shutterstock (bottom).

How to Make Your Houseplants Love You

JOE BAGLEY

THE HOUSEPLANT DOCTOR®

MITCHELL BEAZLEY

Contents

STYLING YOUR PLANTS

PESTS & PROBLEMS

Introduction

Indoor gardening is like an international language: someone who lives in the UK can grow an *Aloe vera* in their home just as easily as someone in Australia. Regardless of where you live, indoor gardeners share the same passion for houseplants.

The benefits of houseplants

My favourite part of horticulture is creating terrariums with small (6cm/2½in) cacti and succulents (see pages 122–129). There are many benefits for growing plants indoors. Here are some of the ways in which creating an indoor oasis benefits our lives.

Numerous studies have found that interacting with plants can lower physiological and psychological stress, improve concentration levels, increase production levels, increase job satisfaction and even remove airborne organic compounds via their roots, soil and leaves.

Helping with mental health

Houseplants (and gardening as a whole) have massively benefited both my mental and physical well-being. Especially during the stresses of my academic years and the sudden passing of my mum when I was 21, I found that tinkering around with plants helped keep my mind on the present instead of the past. There is an old saying about hobbies and mental health: 'Take yourself out of your mind and into your hands.'

No pressure

Finally, never worry about developing your interest in plants, especially if that worry is based on the risk of killing them shortly after purchase. Keep your houseplants by sunless windows, away from any operating radiators, and only water once the top third of the soil dries out. The rest will follow, and you'll slowly gain confidence and new skills.

Two aloes and a *Phalaenopsis* in bloom share a sunny windowsill.

HOW LONG HAVE HOUSEPLANTS BEEN AROUND?

The history of houseplants is interlaced with the history of container gardening. It's full of stories, intrigue and even some controversy. Although there isn't space to delve fully into it here, I definitely recommend investigating this further yourself, as it's fascinating!

A potted history

Around 4,000 years ago in Ancient Egypt, it's believed plants were grown indoors in clay pots filled with nutrient-rich soil from the Nile. In Ancient Greece (1100 bce), it is possible that plants such as bay laurel (*Laurus nobilis*) and palms were planted in the terracotta pots. While in Ancient China it is thought that from around 1000 bce, homes were adorned with plants to symbolize wealth.

During Roman times, container-growing expanded to include flowers, and scented plants such as lavender and rosemary. In cramped towns, people placed plants in window boxes and even on roofs.

Plants on the move

The medieval era (14th century) saw a transfer of temperature-delicate specimens from warmer climes, such as southern Europe, to colder ones, such as northern Europe.

From the 16th to the 18th centuries, the idea of a houseplant developed with the use of conservatories and overseas explorations to the 'New World'. The wealthy filled rooms with citrus trees, while improvements in insulation meant tropical plants became a symbol of affluence. Many houseplants were the product of poaching, where seeds, cuttings or whole plants were taken to another country without the permission of the people in their home nation.

A growing trend

By the end of the 19th century, indoor plants could also be afforded by upper middle-class families. But toxic fumes from the outdoors along with blackening soot produced by domestic heating systems meant they had to choose 'strong' plants, such as the cast iron plant (*Aspidistra elatior*) from eastern Asia and the Kentia palm (*Howea forsteriana*) from Lord Howe Island in the Pacific.

Post-World War II, horticultural businesses, or nurseries, began to hybridize varieties to better tolerate home conditions or to improve aesthetics, such as longer-lasting flowers. During the 1970s and '80s,

The croton, shown here in an illustration from 1882, is a native of Southeast Asia and was introduced to Europe in the 18th century.

CODIAEUM (CROTON) MAGNIFICUM LIND.

it became fashionable to decorate homes with plants that were now available to the masses. Spider plants (*Chlorophytum comosum*) and devil's ivy (*Epipremnum aureum*) hung from macramé pot holders; cheese plants (*Monstera deliciosa*) and rubber plants (*Ficus elastica*) filled the corners of rooms.

Birth of the garden centre

A decade later, the modern garden centre, with cafés and gift shops was born. In more recent times, social media and the pandemic have boosted commercial houseplant growing, proving that humans still need a touch of nature to bring calmness and improve health in a world of rapidly developing technology.

WHERE DO HOUSEPLANTS COME FROM?

Regardless of which plants fill your home, it is good to know where they naturally occur in the wild, as this teaches us what conditions and treatment they like when grown indoors.

For instance, as the native habitats of succulents are in semi-arid environments across the globe, evolution has served them the ability to hold moisture and nutrients in their flesh for long periods of time. This means that for watering them, you should remember the phrase 'drenches between droughts', which, in basic terms, teaches you to wait until the soil is fully dry.

Match their natural habitat

Due to their natural habitat of wet bogs, where soil nutrients are limited, many carnivorous species, such as the popular Venus flytrap (*Dionaea muscipula*) or pitcher (*Sarracenia*), like being sat in water. They also won't tolerate being fertilized, and instead rely on bright sunshine and the occasional bug to digest. This is why you'll never see 'Venus flytrap'-labelled fertilizer in a garden centre!

Boston ferns (*Nephrolepis exaltata*) grow in many regions across the Americas. They have evolved to thrive in high humidity (above 80 per cent) with constant access to soil moisture. Many fern growers keep their ferns standing in a small pool of water to eliminate any chance of dehydration or drought. I've always grown my Boston ferns on bright windowsills with standing water to around one-sixth of the pot's depth. Despite what most sources say, this plant can do very well in partial sun, too. Just make sure the soil never dries out.

Do your research

Take the time to get to know your houseplants and discover where they come from, so you can see how to best mimic the conditions at home. Your houseplants will love you for it!

Top: *Nephrolepis exaltata* growing at the base of a tree. It takes nutrients from the tree sap that trickles down the trunk and is diluted with rainwater.

Bottom left: The yucca's reproductive structure can boast more than 20 flowers at a time.

Bottom right: Three fully-developed *Nepenthes* 'traps' wait for small prey to fall victim to their fragrant, flower-like scents and enter the hollow structures.

HOUSEPLANTS AREN'T JUST FOR CHRISTMAS

Plants can make a brilliant gift as a reminder of a significant event and can be passed down through generations of a family as an incredible inheritance. In fact, some species and varieties of houseplants can live seemingly forever – up to 90 years in some cases. Generally speaking, any species that has the ability to store moisture in either its roots, stems or leaves will be most suitable to become an inheritance. Here are some of my favourites:

Jade tree or Money plant
(*Crassula ovata*)

Commercially grown for over a hundred years, the classic jade plant is the first houseplant to consider if you're interested in creating your own living heirloom. Producing two to three pairs of leaves per year, this species is truly reliable and easy-natured, even for the most inexperienced of indoor gardeners.

Old man cactus
(*Cephalocereus senilis*)

Certainly the hairiest option on this list, the old man cactus could outlive us all. This species will grow around 1cm (½in) per year and can live for at least 40-plus years in the right care. Ensure the specimen is kept in the brightest windowsill in your home, or in a conservatory or semi-heated greenhouse.

Thanksgiving cactus
(*Schlumbergera truncata*)

The third plant I'd recommend is an unalloyed favourite of mine. The traditional idea of a Thanksgiving or Christmas cactus spans back to the 1810s, and although the variety has evolved over the centuries, it still remains a strong seller in garden centres and shops alike.

Cast-iron plant
(*Aspidistra elatior*)

Originating from oriental Asia, this leafier option has been grown in European homes for almost two hundred years due to the species' tolerance to cold, unheated rooms. Cast-iron plants are generally easy to cultivate; however, root rot-related diseases (*Fusarium*) can be a problem.

DO THEY LIKE BEING TALKED TO?

Have you ever thought about singing a sweet lullaby to your plant to make it grow quicker? Well, you would not be alone. Scientists have debated this theory for several decades and the verdicts are rather interesting.

The science

Most studies have found that there could be a correlation between the vibrations created by sound and increased growth rates, but the actual scope of influence is still under discussion. Research conducted in 2007 found that playing 70-decibel music at high frequencies increased cellular and metabolic responses compared to when played at a lower pitch, all at differing speeds. This could be from the plant's mechanoreceptors sensing the vibrational stimuli (of the music, in this case) and preparing it with a defence mechanism to protect it from a natural predator that would eat its leaves in the wild. In other studies, a Canadian research team found that sounds played at 92 decibels to seedlings could be responsible for better germination rates, thereby suggesting that sound vibrations may not only be helping a plant prepare for predation, but also may be a factor for increased growth rates.

The practice

Well, some hypotheses argue that speaking to foliage may help growth due to the sound vibrations, whereas others weigh on the side that a normal conversational volume (and pitch) may not be loud enough to make a clear difference. Either way, if you enjoy talking to your plants or playing them your music, it sure won't hurt them!

Can plants talk back?

Modern research has found that plants can communicate to one another in many different ways. Some use the form of a mycorrhizal network, whereby fungal organisms can communicate messages, nutrients and minerals between trees or plants via the soil and roots. Others, such as grass, send signals into the air after a predator has eaten them to warn other plants in the local vicinity. This signal, which can double up as an invitation to predators to eat the grass-eating insects, is the fragrant smell of a freshly cut lawn that we notice often in the spring and summer months.

Furthermore, scientists have recently found that plants can also make faint popping noises when exposed to dehydration or a damaged stem. These ultrasonic noises can be heard up to 10cm (4in) away and can vary in speed depending on the plant's level of stress.

From left to right: *Zamioculcas zamiifolia, Aglaonema* 'Crete', *Monadenium guentheri, Sansevieria trifasciata* 'Moonshine', *Senecio scaposus, Chlorophytum comosum, Sansevieria cylindrica, Peperomia* 'Rosso', *Goeppertia insignis, Hoya carnosa, Howea forsteriana,* and *Chlorophytum comosum* (under the table).

Right Place,
Right Plant

Just like in a garden, you must select plants that are suitable for the different conditions in your home; some rooms will be exposed to more sunlight than others. It's important to choose drought/sunlight-tolerant species for hot, south-facing rooms or conservatories, and shade-tolerant ones for low-light areas.

What should I know about light levels?

Plants require enough light to produce energy through photosynthesis. The level of light a plant requires depends on its evolution and habitat. Even the brightest areas in your home are darker than the garden, so it's important to know the level of light based on distance from the window. First you need to know the direction in which your rooms face.

North-facing

If you are in the northern hemisphere, a north-facing room is one where the windows point north (and north-west or north-east). These rooms receive minimal sunlight, and are often considered the darkest and coolest. However, a windowsill in a north-facing room is classed as bright, indirect light, meaning that all plants will grow there with no risk of sun-scorch.

East-facing

These rooms provide partial sunlight throughout the day, commonly between 8am and 12pm. During the winter, all houseplants can be grown on these windowsills. For the rest of the year, remove any houseplants that may burn in strengthened sunlight.

South-facing

Rooms that point south-east, south and south-west will be the warmest and brightest. This is especially important for plants kept on second floors or in high-rise apartments, as the chance of trees and other buildings shading the sun will be less likely.

West-facing

Windows that face west provide evening sunlight, and can get quite warm during spring and summer. Only place plants here that can deal with high temperatures and potential dehydration (if you forget to water them), such as herbs, cacti, succulents and carnivorous plants.

South-facing windows and leafy plants

Seasons change, and so too does light intensity. From mid-spring to mid-autumn, a south-facing windowsill (and conservatory) will be too hot for most leafy houseplants. From late autumn to early spring, the sun in a south-facing window becomes weak, so you can relocate tropical plants here. Cacti, succulents and carnivorous plants will be happy to remain on this windowsill throughout the year.

A kitchen windowsill is the ideal place to grow herbs you will cook with. Here they are accompanied by cacti and succulents, including *Sansevieria, Echeveria, Echinocactus grusonii* and an *Opuntia*.

Light levels	Distance from window/areas of house	Specific houseplant care	Recommended plants
Too low (most domestic grow lights are small)	**Windowless room**	Don't water too often, as low-light settings will cause the plant to uptake moisture at slower rates. Feed with each watering using a 'houseplant'-labelled fertilizer.	Small plants are best: • *Fittonia* • *Plectranthus verticillatus* • *Epipremnum aureum* • *Chlorophytum comosum* • *Chamaedorea elegans*
Low light	**North**: More than 2m (6ft) away from any north-facing or partially north-facing windows. On shelves or on tables in the middle of the room. **East, south & west**: Areas that are more than 2.5m (8ft) from the window.	Similarly to windowless rooms, don't water too often, and allow the soil to half-dry out before giving another drink. Use a 'houseplant'-labelled feed each time you water to ensure the plant is well-nourished.	Corners of a shady room: • *Sansevieria trifasciata* 'Laurentii' • *Monstera deliciosa* • *Epipremnum* and *Scindapsus* • *Philodendron erubescens* 'Red Emerald' On shelves: • *Epipremnum* and *Scindapsus* • *Monstera minima* and *M. adansonii* • *Tradescantia zebrina*
Bright, indirect light	**North**: Within 2m (6ft) of a north-west, north or north-east facing window (includes windowsill). **East, south & west**: Being within 1–2m (3–6ft) of a window. **In a conservatory** with a frosted-glass or fabric-covered ceiling.	Perfect for tropical/leafy houseplants. Allow the top third of the soil to dry out in between waters; feel the weight of the pot and rehydrate the potting mix only if it feels lightweight. Try not to place cacti and succulents here due to the lower light levels.	All foliage plants: • Figs • Palms • Crotons • Cordylines • *Sansevierias* • Yuccas • Monsteras • *Pachira aquatica* • Umbrella trees • *Epipremnum* and *Scindapsus* • Pileas • *Fittonia*

Light levels	Distance from window/areas of house	Specific houseplant care	Recommended plants
A spot in a room that has sunlight for up to two hours per day	**East, south & west**: Within 0.5–1m (1½–3ft) of a window. **A position** (in any room) where the sun's rays will hit the plant for up to two hours, before the light levels return to bright, indirect.	Most houseplants can thrive in this area, such as cacti, succulents and carnivorous plants. For tropical/leafy plants, ensure the soil is kept moist during sunny periods (or heatwaves) to avoid dehydration. For cacti and succulents, ensure the soil becomes entirely dry in between waters. These plants are best in sunnier spots.	All foliage plants: • Figs • Palms • Crotons • Cordylines • *Sansevierias* • Philodendrons • Yuccas • Monsteras • *Zamioculcas zamiifolia* • Umbrella trees • *Epipremnum* and *Scindapsus* • Orchids • Pileas
Direct light (sunny)	**East, south & west**: Within 0.5m (1½ft) or closer to a window. Includes being on the windowsill. **In a conservatory** or greenhouse that has a glass ceiling and minimal curtain protection.	Sun-loving plants such as cacti, succulents and carnivorous species will be best suited here. The first two groups will also do well in windowsills (of any compass-facing) where a radiator is operating. Do not place tropical/leafy plants in these areas mid-spring to mid-autumn. Ensure the soil stays moist in warmer rooms (above 20°C/68°F) or when the winter sunlight hits the foliage.	• *Senecio rowleyanus* • *Aloe vera* • *Echeverias* • *Hylotelephium* (previously *Sedum*) • *Kalanchoes* • *Lithops* • Yuccas • *Beaucarnea recurvata* • *Strelitzia reginae* • *Sansevieria trifasciata* • *Cycas revoluta* • All species of cacti and succulents

Is my plant getting enough light?

It's always important to know the signs of a struggling plant and whether inadequate lighting is to blame, so keep reading to learn more.

SYMPTOMS

In most cases, cacti won't show signs of low light and may end up rotting slowly from the base with little warning. Succulents, on the other hand, such as string of pearls (*Senecio rowleyanus*) or jade tree (*Crassula ovata*) will stretch towards the light, meaning that the internodes (or length between the leaves on the stem) will be longer. This is sometimes called 'leggy growth'.

Dark foliage

Most tropical/leafy specimens will develop darker foliage in response to minimal light levels. They'll produce denser chlorophyll to perform more photosynthesis for better energy production. This is why you sometimes see lighter-green monsteras in sunny areas, with deeper-green ones in shadier areas.

Variegation loss

The loss of variegation (patterns on the leaves) is also a symptom of insufficient light. Older leaves' white or lime colours will fade in favour of more chlorophyll (the green pigments of plants), and future growth will more likely sport a fully green appearance.

Root rot

An indirect symptom of low light is root rot. As the photosynthesis levels are lower than they would be in bright areas, the plant won't be up taking as much moisture from the soil. This will result in longer periods of damp soil, which can reduce oxygen levels in the mix and suffocate the root system, resulting in root death.

Why do plants twist towards the light?

Phototropism, which is a process whereby foliage twists towards the light, is not necessarily a sign of ill health and is more to do with optimizing photosynthesis. I wouldn't recommend rotating the plant 180 degrees in dark areas to even out its lean, as it may end up curbing the plant's energy production. Just enjoy it as it is!

The stems of this *Kalanchoe manginii* have twisted towards the light – evidence of phototropism.

How should I care for my plants in low light?

Growing houseplants in dark homes is a different skillset to growing them in brighter houses or in the garden. Although most tropical/leafy houseplants have adapted to thrive in shaded conditions in their natural habitats, our houses are typically much darker, so extra care is needed for success. Here are some simple pointers to successfully growing plants in dim areas.

Only water the soil if it still feels dry to the touch

Double-check if the soil is saturated by feeling the pot's weight: heavy signifies that it's still moist; a light or top-heavy pot needs another drink.

Use tepid water

If the water is too chilly for your teeth, it will shock the plant roots, as well. Lukewarm water or tap water that has been left to sit overnight is best.

Feed when watering

Plants in dark areas won't manufacture as much energy from photosynthesis as they would in brighter spots in the home. To support this process, try mixing in some 'houseplant'-labelled fertilizer with every other watering.

Give your plants a dusting

Every three months, gently hose the leaves in the shower for 15 seconds. This also counts as a watering, so there's no need to rehydrate the soil for a few days afterwards.

Keep it pot-bound

A snug root system will be less likely to suffer from over-watering compared to one that has been transplanted into a too-large pot (or incorrect soil).

Top: A variegated *Monstera* 'Albo' is accompanied by a polka-dot begonia and a *Ctenanthe burle-marxii* 'Amagris'.

Bottom left: A thicket of houseplants sits behind a sofa. It comprises a monstera, butterfly palm and a cane-stemmed begonia.

Bottom right: Sunlight highlights a *Sansevieria trifasciata* and a small terrarium.

Five plants that thrive in low light

Growing (and maintaining) healthy plants kept more than 2m (6ft) away from windows can be a challenge. It can require some skill, as over-watering (and root rot) is a very common problem with low-light conditions. I'd recommend first reading page 18 to learn more about my ultimate dos and don'ts before choosing one of the following plants to fill a shady spot in your home.

Monkey Mask Plant (*Monstera adansonii*)

The *Monstera adansonii* has a similar growth pattern to that of devil's ivy, but different serrations to its foliage. These plants can do very well in low light, even when the curtains are drawn. Take stem cuttings once a year by reducing the vines' overall length by a quarter, to avoid an overly leggy plant.

Chinese evergreens (*Aglaonema*)

These plants have been grown for several decades now as houseplants, but only recently have they become truly popular. Chinese evergreens come in all shapes and sizes, along with some funky variegations and colours. If you choose to grow one of these in a shady spot, be sure to allow all of its soil to dry in between waters – root rot is a common problem for heavy-handed waterers.

Swedish ivy (*Plectranthus verticillatus*)

You'll rarely find this plant in garden centres, so hunting one down can be tricky. Try online for a whole plant or a few cuttings. Is this plant worth the trouble? Absolutely. It will thrive in pretty much every home and any light level. It is drought-tolerant and not too fussy with fertilizer, so it's great for beginners and no-nonsense indoor gardeners.

Mother-in-law's tongue (*Sansevieria trifasciata laurentii*)

Another fantastic plant is *Sansevieria trifasciata* 'Laurentii'. Due to its upright-pointing foliage that will face across the room to the window, they can capture light from quite far away. That's the aim of the game with low-light growing – there's no point purchasing a plant that has leaves only pointing to the ceiling as it will struggle to photosynthesize. As this plant is a desert-dweller, ensure that all of its soil dries in between waters for around two weeks before rehydrating.

Five more plants
- Cast iron plant
  (*Aspidistra elatior*)
- Philodendron erubescens
  (*Philodendron erubescens*)
- Mistletoe cactus
  (*Rhipsalis baccifera*)
- Fishbone cactus
  (*Epiphyllum anguliger*)
- Forest cactus
  (*Lepismium bolivianum*)

Devil's ivy (*Epipremnum aureum*)

This is by far the number-one plant to choose for a dark area. Its versatile growing habit enables you to either hang one over the edge of a shelf, or attach it to nearby walls to grow upwards. Regardless of how you want to showcase your devil's ivy, just make sure that its soil becomes mostly dry in between waters to keep it happy.

Is my plant baking in the sun?

Most tropical/leafy plants can only tolerate a certain amount of direct light per day before damage strikes. If they develop sunburn, it permanently scorches the exposed areas of the plant, so once a leaf develops the typical thin, dehydrated markings that may turn yellow over time, it will remain that colour forever.

THE TWO TYPES OF SUN-SCORCH

There are two ways in which a plant can develop sun-scorch: sudden and gradual. Although a plant won't necessarily die from too much sun, it's important to act quickly to avoid it perishing in the heat. **Sudden scorch** can happen within a few hours and can permanently damage any affected leaf. The plant will eventually develop fresh, healthy growth as long as it has been relocated from the exposed area. **Gradual scorch** can occur over a few weeks or months and won't be as drastic as sudden scorch. The plant may also eventually grow tougher leaves to adapt to the exposed area.

WHAT ARE THE REMEDIES?

Try relocating your plant to a bright area but one less exposed to the sun. Don't immediately place it in a dark area as this will shock the plant (with limited photosynthesis and subsequent plant energy); instead, keep it in a north-facing windowsill for recovery. Keep the affected leaves on the plant unless more than 75 per cent has been damaged, and monitor for new growth at the tips of each stem.

Keeping houseplants outdoors

Ever heard someone say that plants like to be kept outside over summer? Although the outdoors is beneficial for houseplants, placing your plants in a non-shaded area will guarantee sun-scorch within just a few hours. Try keeping them under a tree or garden furniture, or against a north-facing wall, to downplay any risk of burning.

For some species of succulents, such as the *Schlumbergera truncata× bridgesii*, their foliage may turn purple or red when exposed to bright areas. This is to protect the plant from the harsh UV rays emitted by the sun and to avoid subsequent sun-scorch. This doesn't mean the plant needs to be relocated; it is a natural (and awesome) response some species have to adverse conditions.

How do I care for plants in a bright room?

An *Epipremnum aureum* (left), a monstera, *Sansevieria trifasciata* 'Moonshine', fiddle-leaf fig and a peace lily decorate this modern living room.

If you own an apartment or home with large windows, chances are it will get rather bright during the height of summer. There are just a couple of simple things to bear in mind when placing plants in this environment.

An introductory period to its new location
If it's the summer season and you are just about to buy some plants for your apartment, don't overexpose them to the sun immediately. Place them around 1m (3ft) away from a window (either in the middle of the room or up against a wall) for a fortnight or so to acclimatize to

the sun, before placing them in their forever spots. If, however, you have bought plants during autumn, winter or early spring, you can place them in the desired location immediately, without the risk of sun-scorch.

Watering

For cacti and succulents, the best way to hydrate the soil is by following my phrase of 'drenches between droughts'. You should aim for the soil to become fully dry in between drinks by checking the weight of the pot. Only rehydrate the plant if it feels light when lifted; leave for a little longer if it feels heavy.

For sun-loving foliage plants such as yuccas, I would allow most of the soil to dry in between waters by checking moisture levels with your finger.

Flaccid leaves

Many succulents will tell you when they are thirsty by making their older leaves (those closest to the soil on each stem) slightly flaccid.

Five plants that love a sunny spot

During the colder months, you can safely place any houseplant in a sunny window without the risk of sun-scorch. The rays will be weak, but do remember to remove any delicate (shade-loving) plants from this spot from spring onwards – you don't want to be caught out by the intensifying rays.

Spineless yucca (*Yucca elephantipes*)

This yucca can be bought in various heights, ranging from 30cm to 2m (12in to 6½ft). Smaller specimens can be kept in east, south or west-facing windows with ease, while larger ones can be placed within 1m (3ft) of a window or in a conservatory, to instantly add colour to the room. Yellowing lower leaves are a common symptom of insufficient light, so just make sure to read the signs of an unhappy plant and act accordingly.

Silver squill (*Ledebouria socialis*)

The silver squill is one of my favourite houseplants due to its unique variegation – it sports a dark-puce stem with spotted green leaves. In the wild it is found in semi-dry habitats, so be sure to only water its soil once the leaves start to soften over. It's also a bulbed species, meaning you can divide several offsets in the spring to double your stock. It's also an easy houseplant to maintain.

Pelargoniums

These plants, sometimes called 'indoor geraniums', are grown for one of two reasons: either their long-lasting flower habits or their pungent, musty-scented foliage. Regardless of which plant part you love best, pelargoniums are guaranteed to brighten further any sunny window. Feed often and you can expect a perennially blooming plant for minimal care.

Prickly pear cactus (*Opuntia*)

Although these plants are non-toxic, their little spines can sometimes cause skin irritation, so they are best avoided if you have kids or pets. Prickly pears, however, are otherwise fantastic plants to have in bright areas of the home, mostly because of their typical, beautiful, cactus-shaped foliage. If you asked a child to draw a cactus, this is probably what it would look like. Remember to allow all of the soil to dry in between waters – they prefer to be forgotten about!

Tree houseleek (*Aeoniums*)

These are easy to grow due to their tolerance to drought and neglect. Their purple rosette foliage on long, fleshy stems enables the plant to be propagated via stem cuttings. Only water the soil once the oldest leaves (those closest to the soil) begin to soften when pinched. If all of its leaves are plump, water another day!

Five more plants

- Golden barrel cactus (*Echinocactus grusonii*)
- Old man cactus (*Cephalocereus senilis*)
- Mistletoe cactus (*Rhipsalis baccifera*)
- Aloe vera (*Aloe vera*)
- Carnivorous plants (Venus fly traps, pitcher plants, etc) (*Dionaea muscipula, Sarracenia*)

Is my cold porch a no-go area?

When wind or excessive air circulation isn't at play, houseplants do surprisingly well in cold areas of the home. Rooms that are above 15°C (59°F) will be warm enough to support almost all houseplants, whereas there are fewer plants than can tolerate cooler temperatures, and these will need more care.

Dry soil

Remember: you only want to keep the soil on the dry side when the conditions are below 17°C (62°F). Temperatures above this will dry the soil (and plant), so revert to the typical watering regime you use with other plants in warmer rooms. Don't get caught out with dehydration if the room's temperature increases.

A teal-green painted hallway is enhanced by a *Fatsia japonica* on the floor, and various succulents and a yucca on the windowsill above.

1 **Water less often**
Although plants in warm rooms must be kept moist to avoid dehydration, those in cold areas require the opposite. Periods of dry soil are important to avoid root rot, as photosynthesis is lowered in cold conditions, along with moisture evaporation from the soil. Allow most of the soil to dry in between waters, feeling the weight of the pot for lightness. If it's heavy (and the soil feels damp), ignore any watering regimes. The easiest way to kill a houseplant is to water it too often while the temperatures are below 17°C (62°F).

2 **Fertilization is king**
Keeping your green friend well-fed will help it thrive in cooler locations. Potassium is a key element in fertilizers, and it will help harden off a plant, making it more resistant to chilly weather. Feed your plant every second time you water your tropical/leafy houseplant, or every three months for cacti and succulents (see pages 62–66 for more information).

3 **Keep it pot-bound**
Although you may think that giving your plant some more room is beneficial, cold conditions may result in the opposite effect. Plants that have a snug root system in the pot will soak up the moisture in all corners of the potting mix, allowing the soil to dry quicker in between drinks. Those that have been recently repotted into a too-large pot will have a lot of unrooted soil, which will remain wet for long periods of time. These extended periods of moisture will reduce oxygen levels in the soil, which could result in rotten roots.

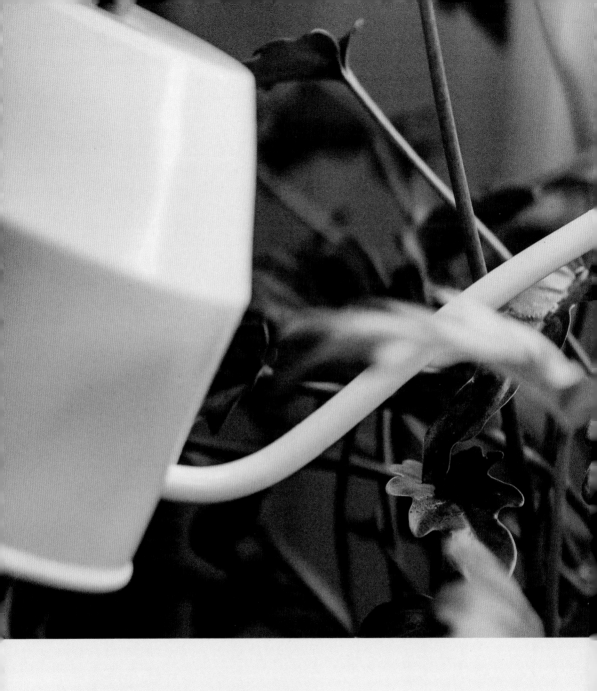

Watering
& Cleaning

Apart from choosing the right place to grow a houseplant, there's one other imperative to learn about indoor growing – hydration. In this section, I'll teach you to know exactly when to water a plant by reading its soil, along with other tips such as root-rot prevention, the type of water to use and leaf hygiene.

How do I ace my watering regime?

A trailing plant grown on a shelf, such as this *Epipremnum aureum,* will dry out slower than it would on a windowsill due to lower light levels. Don't get caught out by watering it too often!

Making sure your plants' watering needs are being met is the most critical element to a happy specimen. Listed below are the key actions you can take. Master the following and you're well on your way to healthy plants.

DO grow plants in pots with drainage.

In the wild, rainfall will naturally drain through the soil via rivulets into deeper portions of the ground, beyond where plant roots cannot access. We can replicate this by growing plants in pots with drainage holes in the base, allowing excess moisture to drain away freely. Never grow directly into a pot without drainage holes, as this will result in waterlogging, which in turn will result in an unhealthy soil and roots.

DO use tepid water.

Ensure your water is at room temperature before applying it to the soil, as cold fluids can reduce photosynthetic rates, making less energy for future growth and overall health. If it's too cold for your pinky finger, it'll be too cold for your plant, too!

DO water your plants more if they're in small pots.

The smaller the pot, the quicker its soil will dry out. If your collection is made up of plants in pots that are 13cm (5in) or smaller, then they'll need watering more often than those in larger pots of 25cm (10in) or more.

DON'T use a heavy potting mix.

Make sure your potting mix is not too water-retentive. 'Heavy' soils that hold moisture for long periods of time are not exclusively bad, but they will decrease the oxygen count in the compost and around the roots. A good example of a heavy soil would be one that consists of a fine potting mix without larger parts such as bark, perlite or pumice. If this is the case with any of your leafy plants (such as peace lilies [*Spathiphyllum wallisii*], monsteras, devil's ivy [*Epipremnum aureum*]), be sure to replace the soil with a potting mix that contains the components mentioned above.

DON'T water too often if your room is cold.

Rooms that are set at a temperature below 18°C (64°F) will slow down the rate at which soil dries and photosynthesis takes place, making your plant less thirsty.

DON'T water your plants in a dark location as frequently.

Similar to cool temperatures, low light levels will reduce the photosynthetic rates and lessen the need for constant watering. An indoor shady location is more than 2m (6ft) from a window.

Recycle a water bottle

Why not water your plants with an old water bottle? Apart from the benefits of 'reduce, reuse, recycle', it enables you to see how much of the bottle you pour into each pot without having to guess with watering cans. Have a go and see if it works for you!

Should I use a particular type of water?

Among gardeners and houseplant growers alike, there's a lot of chat about which type of water is best for houseplants. You'll find people online questioning whether 'chlorine will damage my plant over time' or if 'de-ionized water is better than tap water'. The answers are simple, so let me explain...

TAP WATER

While containing fluoride and chlorine that some believe harm plants, in most areas tap water is safe to use with houseplants. Although using water straight from the tap won't necessarily hurt your plant, let it sit for 6–12 hours to both settle the chlorine levels and increase its overall temperature. High levels of chlorine will reduce the microbial activity within soil for around 36 hours, whereas cold water may cause a sudden dip in photosynthesis rates.

If you want to go the extra mile and be sure your tap water won't hurt your plant, check it provides pH levels of around 6–7 (you can buy pH testing kits online). For readings outside this bracket, contact your local water management company, who should provide more information.

Soft vs hard water

Softened water should be avoided long term due to the risk of sodium build-up in the soil that can result in moisture-uptake distortion. Hard water may also provide negatives in the likes of pH level changes and nutrient uptake in the plant. See the other water sources listed below for viable alternatives.

OTHER WATER SOURCES
Collected rainwater

As long as you don't use stagnant water, rainwater is the cheapest and best way to hydrate a houseplant. Generally, it is naturally the correct pH for them, but it isn't recommended for seeds or seedlings as their resistance to disease and bacteria is limited until they reach maturity.

Spring water

Although a relatively expensive option, spring water contains naturally occurring minerals such as calcium, magnesium and fluoride. These will help the plant regulate certain behaviours and overall health. Run the water through a carbon filter to remove excess minerals before using a fertilizer that contains calcium and magnesium, to alleviate the two elements' natural deficit.

Disused aquatic tank water

Some growers hydrate their plants using disused aquatic water from domestic fish tanks, which contains higher levels of nitrogen. Similarly to rainwater, only use this type of water on mature houseplants and not on seedlings or carnivorous plants.

Watering a *Ficus elastica*. An *Asplenium nidus* (bottom) and a *Epipremnum aureum* (top) are waiting for a drink.

Water that helps to feed your plants

Both distilled and de-ionized water may leach (remove) nutrients from the soil, essentially fighting with the plants for nutrients. While these waters won't kill your plants, they may pose a challenge to them if you don't regularly use a fertilizer. Purified water is, however, fantastic to hydrate sensitive groups of plants such as carnivorous ones, where soil fertilization is not needed as much, as they obtain their food from catching small insects.

How do I know if my plant is thirsty?

One of the ways I manage my four hundred-odd houseplants is by checking certain plants each morning. This doesn't always mean picking the plant up or checking its soil, it can be a simple case of glancing over it for signs of wilting or curling leaves.

HOW DO I CHECK FOR DRY SOIL?

Prioritize checking any plants that are grown in pots narrower than 10cm (4in) in diameter, as these will dry quickly due to the small volume of soil. Plants within 1m (3ft) of an operating heater or large, floor-to-ceiling windows (in flats, etc.) should also be prioritized.

HOW MUCH WATER SHOULD I USE?

Aim to add water slowly into all 'four corners' of the pot until it begins to drain from the hole in the base. Observe the drainage holes: once the fluid drains out from the bottom, it's time to stop. If you want to drain more moisture from the soil, stand the pot at a slight angle for five minutes. This will concentrate the drainage in one area.

SHOULD I USE A WATERING GLOBE OR MOISTOMETER?

Glass watering globes are best used in pots with a diameter of 15cm (6in) or larger. I recommend them for plants that are grown within 1m (3ft) of a windowsill, as promoting continual soil moisture in low-light areas could cause root rot. Moistometers aren't as useful. Although these can help identify dry compost, this is rather subjective as one person's perception of a '7/10 moisture' reading might be wetter than another's.

Fresh soil will hold water

If your plant dries out often, why not repot it into the next size of pot (with drainage holes) and a fresh batch of soil? Surrounding a root system with new potting mix will downplay the rate of dehydration. Flick to page 70 to learn more!

ARE THERE ANY PLANTS I CAN IGNORE?

Plants grown in pots wider than 25cm (10in), as well as drought-tolerant species, are fine to ignore for a couple of weeks. Plants such as cacti and succulents, those enclosed in terrariums and any houseplants kept more than 2m (6ft) from a window or on a shelf shouldn't need hydrating regularly. Check out page 48 for five plants you can neglect.

AM I USING THE CORRECT AMOUNT OF WATER?

If you're someone who prefers to use a specific amount of water, here are a few numbers to note:

Don't worry about giving a plant too much water in one go. As long as the pot has drainage holes, any excess moisture it can't hold on to will drain away. You can always sit the potted plant at a 45-degree angle, to encourage any remaining excess water to drip out of the container.

If, however, you're growing a plant in a pot without any holes, you must water it a little and often, instead of drenching it as described above. I'd recommend watering your non-drained potted plants with only one-quarter of the amount of water recommended below, once every week or so.

Pot sizes (diameter)	Amount of water to give
1–7cm (½–2¾in)	65ml (3fl oz)
7.1cm – 10cm (2¾in–4in)	150ml (5fl oz)
10.1cm – 12cm (4–4¾in)	275ml (10fl oz)
12.1cm – 15cm (4¾–6in)	425ml (15fl oz)
15.1cm – 20cm (6–8in)	500ml (16fl oz)
20.1cm – 25cm (8–10in)	800ml (1.6 pints)
25.1cm – 30cm (10–12in)	1300ml (2.3 pints)
30.1cm – 40cm (12–16in.)	1600ml (2.5 pints)
40.1cm + (16in +)	2000ml (3.5 pints)

Why is my plant wilting?

Wilting is not just a symptom of dehydration – in serious cases of over-watering, the entire root system will fail and reduce the ability to uptake water from the soil, causing the plant to wilt. Before you panic, it doesn't necessarily mean the plant will die. In most cases it can be caught early and a simple drink of water will be the remedy.

To find out if your plant is thirsty or suffering from over-watering, start by checking the smell, colour and texture of the potting mix.

Dehydrated soil
– Generally lighter in tone
– No smell
– Crumbly or hardened
– The soil and rootball feel loose in the pot

Over-watered soil (root rot)
– Generally darker in tone
– Earthy smell
– Saturated soil that clumps together
– Fungus gnats, soil mould and/or fungus present
  (these are not detrimental to your plant)

Check for holes

If the pot doesn't have drainage holes, it's a good indicator that over-watering could be the issue.

Having checked the soil, if you're confident your plant is over-watered, turn to page 50; if you think it's dehydrated, turn to page 46. If, however, you're still a little unsure, simply take the plant out of the pot and glance over the outer edge of its rootball. Try not to over-touch the roots or pull soil from them as this may result in 'transplant shock' (see page 74). Most root systems are plump, light coloured and cannot be pulled off easily from the plant. Root rot is often the complete opposite.

A *Ctenanthe burle-marxii* is repotted into a ceramic pot with drainage holes in the base.

I forgot my plant existed – how can I save it?

It's good to know that even with a serious case of dehydration, where the leaves are brown or crispy, there are still ways to save the legacy of the plant via cuttings. Propagating a dying plant is like jumping from a sinking ship – the cuttings live on, even if the mother plant does not.

Work through the following steps and decide whether propagation is necessary to keep your plant's legacy alive.

STEPS TO REHYDRATE

1 In the shower or bathtub, with the plant still in its pot, hose the foliage thoroughly until the leaves drip with water, and ensure the soil is moist, too.

2 Take a picture of the plant while it's wilting and compare it 24 hours later to check its progress. During this time, you can either keep the plant in the bathroom, or place it in another humid area of the house to recover.

THE PLANT HAS STOPPED WILTING

The plant should be out of danger if its foliage is still mostly green. Prune off any browning, yellowing or crisping leaves to improve its overall appearance.

Finally, consider repotting the plant into the next-sized pot, with drainage holes. A fresh band of soil around its rootball will act as a water reserve to downplay the risk of another drought. Ensure the plant isn't being grown in too much sun or near an operating radiator and relocate if necessary.

Cut your losses

If your plant continues to wilt even after four days, its ability to uptake moisture from the soil has been severely affected. See pages 82–91 for advice on taking cuttings and plant propagation.

A shelving unit holds trailing plants including a *Epipremnum aureum*, while a *Peperomia argyreia* and *Beaucarnea recurvata* complete the display.

Five plants you can neglect

When you hear the words 'plant neglect', you may think of a bad plant parent. However, some plants will prefer to be forgotten about due to their impressive tolerance to long periods of dry soil. The following five plants I recommend here are my go-to for people who either work away from home, jet off to somewhere warm frequently or simply forget to tend to their plants often!

Pineapple plant (*Ananas comosus*)

Pineapple plants are a great option for those wanting something unusual in the home, along with kids who eventually want to grow their own fruits. The plant can tolerate occasional droughts and forgetful feeding regimes, so you shouldn't have to worry about coming home to a withering plant. Water once every 10 to 14 days and provide a sunny windowsill (upstairs rooms are best due to the warmer temperatures that they like).

Jade plant (*Crassula ovata*)

A member of the succulent family, jade plants are an excellent choice for any windowsill that you may own. Their fleshy stems and leaves make them a great drought tolerator, holding moisture for weeks (and even months) at a time. Only rehydrate your jade plant once the oldest leaves (those closest to the soil along the stems) become soft or wrinkly.

Natal lily (*Clivia miniata*)

Clivias produce bold, orange, trumpet-shaped flowers in the spring or summer, along with year-round fleshy, glossy leaves. They can be happy without water for over a month and still not look wilted or sad. Clivia are perfect for 'medium-light' areas of the home, which include sunless windowsills, or on furniture that's up to 2.5m (8ft) away from a window.

Cast iron plant (*Aspidistra elatior*)

This plant can grow in the darkest of homes and still look a million dollars, but the one thing it can't tolerate is over-watering. Its thick rhizomes hold moisture for long periods, so constant watering is frowned upon. Place it in any location in your home except full sun, and only water once the soil becomes fully dry.

Five more plants

- Dragon trees (*Dracaena*)
- Polka Dot Begonia (*Begonia maculata*)
- African milk bush (*Euphorbia trigona*)
- Ponytail palm (*Beaucarnea recurvata*)
- Ladyfinger cactus (*Mammillaria elongata*)

ZZ plant (*Zamioculcas zamiifolia*)

This is the true definition of a neglect-tolerant species. Its roots, bulbs (called 'tubers') and leaves are bursting with moisture. With this in mind, it's best kept dry for around a month before another water, which is usually enough time to sneak away for a quick holiday in the sun.

Have I over-watered my plant?

It's a common misconception that pouring too much water during one hydration will cause root rot, but if your potting mix is of a good quality, it will hold on to a certain amount of moisture before letting go of excess through the pot's drainage holes. As long as you give the soil a rest between drinks, you needn't worry about giving your plants too much water.

If you do over-water, it is usually caused by either rehydrating the soil too often within a short timeframe, or if the pot lacks holes in the bottom, causing a pool to accumulate within the compost. Here's my advice for spotting the tell-tale signs and how to restore a waterlogged plant to life.

Top: Watering a *Thaumatophyllum bipinnatifidum*.

Bottom left: This *Spathiphyllum wallisii* shows the typical damage of over-watering – the symptoms of root rot, including wilting, brown or yellow leaves.

Bottom right: A *Dieffenbachia* with an abnormal amount of yellowing leaves due to over-watering. The leaves should be removed.

SYMPTOMS OF OVER-WATERING
Stems and leaves
Wilting
Dehydrated or deflated leaves (most likely with succulents)
Rapid yellowing of leaves
Older leaves drop off easily
A rotten base of stem (most likely with succulents)

Soil and root system
Soil is dark-toned and clumpy
Soil smells earthy
White mould on the soil
Adult fungus gnats and their larvae are present
Deflated, collapsed or squishy roots that can be easily pulled off from the rootball

STEPS TO SAVE AN OVER-WATERED PLANT

If you suspect your plant has been over-watered, follow these steps:

1 Gently take the plant out of the pot and inspect the root system. Try not to over-touch it or pull soil from the plant as it will result in transplant shock (see page 74). For now, look for cream or light-coloured roots that should be plump and three-dimensional.

An *Epipremnum aureum* being repotted into a terracotta pot.

2 If the roots are collapsed, rotten and smell earthy, then gently tug on a singular root to see if it will pull off easily. If so, work through the outer edge of the rootball by gently feeling each root strand to see if it is alive. Note: In some cases, only certain sections of the rootball will rot, so be careful not to remove healthy parts!

If all of the roots are rotten: If there are no healthy roots, the best way to save the plant's legacy is by taking stem cuttings (see page 85). Research online or in a book and follow the recommendations on propagation. Cut the stem as if the plant were healthy. Discard the bottom parts of the houseplant.

1 Once you have worked through the healthy and rotten roots, hold the stem in one hand and gently shake the rootball. This will release the affected soil and any final dead roots from the plant. Rinse the rootball with lukewarm water for around a minute. You can also use rooting gels and powders, as I find that these help to stimulate the root system.

2 Choose a 'houseplant'-labelled potting mix or sphagnum moss and a pot – with drainage holes – that is 2cm (1in) wider than the rootball. Fill the bottom quarter of the pot with soil or moss and place the plant on top. Pour soil or moss around the gaps between the roots and pot until you reach three-quarters of the pot's height.

3 Pour lukewarm water with a 'houseplant'-labelled fertilizer through the potting mix until it drips through the drainage holes. Place in a bright, sunless windowsill and wrap the pot (and plant) in a transparent box or bag with several holes for ventilation. The air around the plant will be humid from the soil and will urge the plant to provide new root and leaf growth, eventually! Hydrate the soil as necessary.

How should I water cacti and succulents?

Keeping your cacti or succulents happily hydrated requires a slightly different mindset compared to the usual tropical plants of *Monstera* or *Syngonium*.

WHY THEIR NATURAL HABITAT MATTERS

Due to harsh conditions found in their natural habitats, these desert dwellers have adapted to hold moisture in their roots, stems or leaves for photosynthesis. Many species grow naturally in leaching soils, where rainwater and nutrients drain quickly through the ground and out of reach of their root systems. Their habitats are essentially a continuous drought that is divided by sudden downpours occurring every few weeks or months.

JOE'S CATCHY WATERING TIP

Think of my simple phrase of 'drenches between droughts' when considering your plant's next drink.

Only rehydrate your plant's soil once it becomes entirely dry. You can tell this either by feeling the soil with your fingers or by assessing the pot's weight. If the soil feels moist or the pot is heavy, there is enough moisture to keep your prickly friend happy.

When your plant needs watering, keep pouring lukewarm water into the soil until it drains through the pot's drainage holes, to ensure it's thoroughly irrigated. Allow it to drain for five minutes before returning it to its usual spot in your home.

A KEY FACTOR THAT WILL DELAY DRYING SOIL

This relates to your room's temperature: cacti and succulents are surprisingly good at enduring cold temperatures below 6°C (42°F) as their natural habitats may dip during the night or in high winds. Between the months of mid-autumn and early spring, I recommend a period of five weeks in between watering succulents, while extending this further to every eight weeks for cacti. Remember: less is more during the chillier months.

Rehydrate
The best time to rehydrate a jade plant or aloe vera is when their oldest leaves (those that are closest to the soil on each individual stem) begin to soften over slightly. Thirsty Thanksgiving and Christmas cacti are the opposite as their newest/youngest leaves will become floppy when needing a drink.

Succulents, including *Crassula ovata* 'Hummel's Sunset', *Echeveria* 'Miranda', *Senecio cephalophorus*, *Pilosocereus pachycladus* and *Haworthiopsis*.

Top tip
Don't water a desert dweller with the mindset of 'little and often', as this will promote continuous soil moisture that may result in root rot.

Can I put my plants in the shower?

There are people who shower with their plants. Is this rather peculiar activity beneficial for the foliage, or just an old wives' tale? I'll bare all here...

WHAT ARE THE BENEFITS?

The water spray from the shower removes dust from the foliage, which in turn increases photosynthesis (and, therefore, provides more energy for the plant to grow). A quick shower will improve the overall vigour of your plant, making it look brand new within seconds. Most of our houseplants are from tropical regions, so an occasional spell in the shower will replicate rainfall and hydrate leaves.

Which plants will thank you?

Plants such as *Alocasia*, *Anthurium*, ferns, *Sansevieria*, *Monstera*, palms and peace lilies (*Spathiphyllum wallisii*) are big fans of an occasional visit to the shower cubicle, along with all other tropical/leaf plants. Cacti, succulents and other desert dwellers will benefit from a quick rinse, but only once or twice a year (once in autumn and once in spring is ideal), to avoid moisture resting in their stems' cubbyholes, which can cause rot.

PLANT SHOWERS ARE AS EASY AS 1-2-3

Two Epipremnum aureum (left) and two Philodendron hederaceum (right) are at home in this shower cubicle.

1   The best time to rinse a houseplant is when its soil has become dry after its last water. Due to the spray inadvertently saturating the compost, your green friend's roots will have a good drink. See page 42 to check the signs of a dry soil.

2   Place your plant into the shower cubicle (still in its pot) and ensure the water temperature is warm. Hose the foliage for 15 seconds; you will only need to spritz each leaf.

3   Turn off the water supply and give the plant a ten-second shake, then leave it in the cubicle until the foliage is dry again. Although there is no limit to how often you can shower a plant, four times a year (every three months) will keep it looking fresh.

Tap or hose

If your plant is small, use the kitchen tap to freshen up its leaves. Any specimen too big for your shower cubicle can be rinsed gently outside using a garden hose, but only when outdoor temperatures are above 18°C (64°F).

Is leaf-shine spray good for them?

The debate over whether leaf-shining products are appropriate for a plant's wellness has been a hot topic for decades. Can you safely use these gas-canister items on your foliage, or should you avoid them? Here I have the answer, and a surprisingly easy alternative.

WHY LEAF-SHINE PRODUCTS ARE NOT HEALTHY

Products that improve a plant's twinkle using a gas canister should be avoided for two reasons. Firstly, they can block the stomata (where the plant 'breathes' from), limiting photosynthesis and future energy production levels. There are also opinions that a too-shiny leaf can reflect light away from the leaf before it can process it, especially plants kept in dark areas of the home. Although your green friend may look dazzling, this type of product puts appearance before health, so it's best to avoid it. Plants within the orchid or aroid families (alocasias, peace lilies [*Spathiphyllum wallisii*] and monstera) will be most affected due to stomata being located on both sides of the leaf.

ARE THERE ANY ALTERNATIVES?

In terms of leaf cleanliness, there is a much more straightforward remedy: water. While it may sound like a killjoy, most plants will enjoy a quick wipe-down of their leaves with a warm, wet cloth or a spritz in the shower. If you're looking for something to use after wiping the foliage, try 'Photo+'. Although not strictly for the glossiness of the foliage, products like this will promote better rates of photosynthesis, improve foliage growth, and will even strengthen the plant against pests and diseases.

Milk and oils

I've heard people recommending milk or oils to improve their plants' brilliance, but these may do more harm than good. They won't pose much of a threat in terms of toxicity, but they may cause the foliage to become sticky, thereby collecting dust at a quicker rate. 'Stick to water' is what I say!

Looking closely at its leaves shows the textures and morphology of different plant species.

Top left: *Spathiphyllum wallisii.*

Top right: *Anthurium andraeanum.*

Bottom left: Monstera.

Bottom right: *Alocasia* × *amazonica.*

Feeding, Repotting & Making New Plants

The basics of plant nutrition, repotting and propagation
are straightforward if you follow my guide on the following
pages. If you're new to plants, don't panic! These terms may
be new to you, but you'll get the hang of them in due course.

Do I need to feed my plants?

In their natural biomes, plants have seemingly unlimited nutrient sources and space for their roots to grow. Systems such as the nitrogen cycle and nutrient uptake in the roots, and external factors (worms, fungi and microbial activity), all help a plant thrive. But what happens when a plant is kept in a pot and all natural processes are stripped away?

BENEFITS OF FERTILIZATION

The primary use for a fertilizer is to replicate the nutrients typically available in the natural world but in the pot instead. Like humans, houseplants need a balanced diet of nutrients and minerals to thrive. There are 17 elements a plant needs, with the main three being nitrogen, phosphorus and potassium (NPK).

Apart from replenishing nutrients taken up by the plant, fertilizers can also help improve the *soil's* overall health. Ensuring your compost is healthy on a microbial level is just as important as keeping a plant in tiptop condition, but how can you do this? You can use organic-based feeds, along with repotting your plants with organic-rich material, such as bark and worm castings.

WHAT IF I NEVER FERTILIZE MY PLANTS?

This question largely falls on how much light your plant receives. Although there are other factors, such as the quality of soil you used and the species of plant, most of the time the plant will survive (instead of thrive). Regular fertilization will help minimise pest and disease damage, along with aiding photosynthesis rates and soil health, which both fuel a plant's long-term success. A specimen that is grown in a sufficiently lit room or windowsill will be 'nourished' by the sunlight when it is converted into glucose, so this is, at least, something that will keep the plant alive. The species itself can also play a role, as with cacti and succulents, which have adapted to survive with minimal nutrients in the soil.

Two side tables of differing heights host an array of houseplants. From left to right: *Dieffenbachia, Alocasia × amazonica, Senecio cephalophorus, Clusia rosea, Echeveria* or *Pachyphytum*, an aloe, avocado, two air plants, a hanging *Tradescantia* and a *Heptapleurum*.

TYPES OF FERTILIZERS
Mineral/salt
With this type of feed, the minerals are mined to contain the essential plant nutrients for optimal growth. Although it is good for promoting new foliage and flowers, the soil health may not benefit from solely using these feeds, so it's important to incorporate an organic feed, too.

Organic
This feed is based on plant matter and organic compounds, which can benefit the structure, oxygenation and microbial activity of the soil. Most organic fertilizers contain seaweed extract, which is a natural bio-stimulant and contains auxin for growth regulation. Some also have humic acids that will further help the plant and soil.

A large difference between a mineral fertilizer and an organic alternative is that the former is mined from limestone rock phosphate (and not necessarily natural) but is quickly bioavailable for the plant, whereas the latter's nutrients have to be broken down (by microbes), which can take time. Have a go at swapping between a mineral-based feed on one occasion, then an organic feed on the second. Keep swapping to help both the soil and plant when it's time to fertilize.

Biorational
New technologies and research have highlighted the importance of soil microbial health for houseplants. Indoor plants benefit from a solid relationship with their compost via a natural symbiosis between the fungi, bacteria and other microbes that live around and interact with the root system. Biorational fertilizers are the best of both worlds in terms of meeting nutrient needs for a plant as well as nurturing the biological needs of the soil. Using a simple product on its own mixed with water (without using other fertilizers) is the best way to replicate the plant's natural soil biology and nutrient demands indoors.

WHERE DO I START WITH FEEDING MY PLANTS?
This page has a lot of funky buzzwords that describe how a plant needs to be fed. But the 'art' of fertilization is just as easy as watering a plant – and you can do that already!

I recommend a 'biorational houseplant fertilizer' that benefits the plant and its soil. You'll only need around 2ml (0.07oz) of feed per litre (35fl oz) of water, so a small bottle will go a long way. I feed my plants every second water – usually every 14 days, depending on the species.

The corner of a room is filled with *Epipremnum aureum*, *Asparagus setaceus*, *Platycerium*, *Araucaria heterophylla*, *Crassula* 'Hobbit' and *Sansevieria trifasciata*.

What do I need to know about soil?

If I were to emphasize one critical thing that will guarantee to help a plant's success, it would be a healthy potting mix. I don't just mean using a good-quality soil, but also ensuring it is well-structured and fed with a specific feed is crucial for a strong relationship between the compost and a root system (see page 62 for advice on feeding).

SOIL STRUCTURE: WHAT DOES IT MEAN?

I'm sure you've heard of the benefits of a well-structured potting mix. Different ingredients used in soils have different roles to play, from promoting airflow to increasing drainage for sensitive species.

Coconut coir: The base that will make the main consistency of the mix.

Perlite: Aids drainage and oxygenation. Rice hulls are an eco-friendly alternative.

Bark/orchid bark: Helps with drainage, soil structure and microbial activity.

Grit: For drainage and to weigh down the soil, in case your plant is top-heavy.

Sand: For drainage and, sometimes, oxygenation of the soil.

Pumice: Improves soil structure and promotes aeration around the root system.

Care for carnivores

Carnivorous plants such as Venus flytraps (*Dionaea muscipula*) and pitchers will need specialist 'carnivorous' soil. Most soils will be too nutrient-rich for them, which results in root-burn and in some cases, death. These special soils replicate the bogs and conditions that most insect-eating plants would interact with in the wild.

Worm castings: Provides soil structure and nutrients for the plant; helps with bioactivity.

Activated charcoal/carbon: Helps hold nutrients in the soil; increases moisture retention.

Sphagnum moss: Retains moisture and improves aeration in a terrarium or growing cuttings.

QUICK SOIL RECIPES USING PRODUCTS FROM A GARDEN CENTRE

Most of the products you'll need for a well-structured houseplant medium will be in your local plant shop, with only a few needing to be bought online (worm castings, for example). Try the following:

Desert dwellers
For cacti and succulents
— 1 part 'John Innes No.2'
— 0.5 part perlite
— 1 part grit
— 0.25 part worm castings (optional)

Jungle potting mix
Especially for: *Epipremnum aureum, Monstera, Philodendron, Syngonium, Dieffenbachia, Aglaonema, Anthurium*
— 2 parts coconut coir
— 1.5 parts perlite (or rice hulls)
— 0.75 part worm castings
— 1.75 parts bark
— 0.5 part activated charcoal

Houseplant potting mix
A multipurpose medium for most repotting adventures, most houseplants and seed sowing.
— 2 parts coconut coir
— 1.5 parts perlite (or rice hulls)
— 0.75 part worm castings

What if the soil is rock solid?

Hardened soil is often over-looked or ignored by houseplant growers. It's usually a gradual process, but it can be exacerbated by constant dehydration from overly sunny or hot rooms. Cacti and succulents are most likely to develop an overly dehydrated rootball, but is it actually bad for a plant?

WHAT CAUSES HARD SOIL?

Desert dwellers and those that prefer drier conditions can sometimes 'hug' and squeeze the soil through their roots to eke out all last remnants of moisture. It's a natural behaviour and shouldn't cause concern if the compost is flaky and loose. However, when the soil has become so hard that moisture runs straight over the rootball – known as 'hydrophobic soil' – this should be addressed to avoid the plant developing water-stress.

Note that a potting mix will compact over time anyway, especially when the plant is kept in the same pot for more than five years.

SYMPTOMS OF HYDROPHOBIC SOIL

Look for hardened compost that's hard to break up with your fingers and check that water doesn't sit on top (instead of draining quickly through). Other tell-tale signs are that the soil/plant rattles in the pot and has small gaps between the pot's inside edge and the rootball, or the plant still looks dehydrated, even a few days after watering it.

WHAT CAN I DO TO LOOSEN THE SOIL?

First, submerge the plant in water around 30 per cent in depth and leave for an hour. Then, take the plant out of its pot and gently loosen the rootball (roots and soil) with your fingers. The best way to do this is by placing your fingers in the very centre of the rootball's bottom face and teasing the bottom edges to splay outwards. Remember not to pull soil from the roots and instead just try to break into the hardiness of its soil.

Finally, repot the plant into the next-sized pot (usually up to 3cm/1in bigger in diameter) and use a suitable potting mix. Turn to pages 70–73 and continue from step 6 of the step by step guide on repotting.

How to avoid hard soil in the future

Avoid dehydrating the soil for too-long periods in between drinks. When the roots are exposed to a reliable watering schedule that doesn't promote long droughts, the roots won't have the urge to squeeze the potting mix in search of moisture. Ensure you repot any houseplants that are grown in pots smaller than 12cm (5in) in diameter every two years, to further avoid a hardening soil profile.

An aloe being transferred to a new pot. This is what a healthy succulent root system looks like.

Care for the elderly

The steps here can also be used for old inherited houseplants that may need some TLC from being in the same pot. Be careful with aged plants, as they can be more sensitive to transplant shock, so it's best to loosen only the bottom quarter of the rootball instead of the whole area.

How do I repot my plant?

Repotting can be daunting, especially if you're new to the game. For anyone panicking: stop, and relax for a second. Unless your plant has root rot, you don't need to rush into repotting it immediately. You're more likely to hurt the plant by cutting corners or wrongly handling its rootball, so keep reading for some dos and don'ts on repotting, along with a definitive guide to successful transplantation.

DO water the plant before repotting.

To lower the risk of transplant shock, water the plant a few hours before repotting (while still in its original pot). Dry root systems can sometimes be susceptible to damage, resulting in yellowed foliage, stunted growth and wilting.

DO be gentle with the rootball.

Always treat the rootball with respect. Loosening off the bottom 20 per cent is beneficial for post-repotting growth, but too much touching will weaken the plant.

DO have fun!

Take your time and have fun! Repotting usually takes around ten minutes, which is the perfect time to drift away from daily stresses.

DON'T over touch the roots.

Handle the rootball carefully. Especially with older houseplants (five years old or more), it's important not to over-touch the roots by pulling soil from them or loosening them up too much. (More on this later.)

DON'T push the new compost down.

Once the plant is sat in its new pot with fresh soil, avoid pushing the compost down to aid plant stability. This is a bad practice, mostly because of the risk of lowering air circulation around the roots. Watering the plant will consolidate the soil sufficiently and help settle the roots into their new home.

DON'T compact the soil

If your plant is toppling over, use a support cane or moss pole (for trailing plants) to keep it upright. Gently apply some pressure around the cane's base to aid stability, but never go overboard with soil compaction.

Alocasia × *amazonica* being repotted. Beside it are an already-repotted *Dieffenbachia* and a *Spathiphyllum wallisii.*

Plant health check

Repotting a plant is the perfect time to check for root rot, and critters such as fungus gnats and root mealybugs.

HOW TO REPOT

1 While wearing a pair of gloves and in a well-ventilated space, take the plant out of the pot to inspect the soil and root system. If you find it hard to remove the pot, carefully cut a plastic pot with secateurs, or gently crack and dismantle it with a hammer if it's made of ceramic/terracotta.

2 Investigate for root rot, as this must be dealt with immediately before the transplant (see page 166 for symptoms and remedies). Plants often have a few dead root strands. If more than 10 per cent of the roots have died, turn to page 74.

3 Loosen the fresh, new potting mix. Break up the soil until it becomes 'friable' (a fancy word that basically means 'fluffy').

4 Loosen off the bottom fifth of your plant's rootball, so that the roots can explore the new soil freely. Place your finger in the centre of the rootball's bottom face, and tease the bottom edges to splay outwards.

5 Fill the bottom fifth of the new pot with the fresh potting mix and rest the rootball on top. Continue to fill the gap between the rootball's edge and the pot's inner side until you reach the same height as the original soil.

6 Sprinkle a final layer of soil over the new potting mix – around 3cm (1in). Remember, you want the pot's top lip to remain above the soil line, to avoid any run-off when watered. Try not to pat the soil down with your hands. Pushing down will overly compact the soil and promote an anaerobic condition where air cannot freely move within the potting mix and root system.

7 Place the potted plant onto a flat surface and tap the side of the pot to lightly compact the compost's structure. If the plant needs support, provide a stake, trellis or moss pole. After the first hydration, the water hitting the fresh soil may cause it to develop a few craters. Simply refill any dips with more compost, or re-level it with the pre-existing soil.

Loosening soil

Especially with mature houseplants (more than ten years old), the old soil might be hard, like a brick. It's best to loosen off such rootballs slightly by following the tips on page 69. Once you have completed the recommended steps there, return to this page and follow step 6 onwards.

AFTERCARE

Due to the rootball being wrapped around fresh compost, you may not need to water the plant as often as you are used to doing. Keep an eye on the moisture levels by feeling the weight of the pot. If it feels light and easily movable when lifted, it's time for a drink! Monitor your plant's progression. Check for wilting, stunted growth and other symptoms that may be the result of transplant shock (see page 74). Although it takes a month or two for specimens to settle into their new home, they will eventually reward you with healthy growth.

Top: Soil is added to the top of a repotted *Sansevieria trifasciata* 'Laurentii' to level out the top layer of the soil.

Bottom: This *Sansevieria trifasciata* 'Laurentii' has a healthy root system.

Why does my plant not like its new pot?

After being repotted, it's good to know that if a plant takes time to respond with new leaves it hasn't necessarily become stressed or unwell. Plants have different growth rates, so never panic if your plant seems frozen in time after a transplant. However, there are reasons why a plant is unhappy in its pot.

1 Transplant shock

Symptoms: Curled, floppy leaves, often accompanied by rapidly yellowing foliage.

Cause: Heavy-handedness with the roots while repotting.

Remedy: Turn to page 166 to learn more on what to do next.

2 Anaerobic soil (root rot)

Symptoms: Damaged root system over the course of a few weeks. Once the roots start to decay, the plant stops producing new growth. The leaves will become floppy or curled, with the soil smelling earthy and feeling water-laden.

Causes: Keeping the soil too moist in between drinks (see page 42 to learn how to correctly water a plant); over-potting in a too-large container.

Remedy: Turn to page 166 to learn more on what to do next.

3 The flowers on my plant have suddenly fallen off

Symptoms: Within two weeks of repotting, the flowers drop off with no prior warning. Other flowers may wilt or collapse and will look dehydrated before falling off.

Cause: This is a side-symptom of transplant shock but is most prevalent with plants that are in flower when repotted.

Remedy: For orchids, prune the flower stalk back to around half, just 2cm (1in) above a non-flowered node. This will look like a raised bump on the stem that has a slight point to it. Keep the orchid in its original spot in your home and wait for a fresh flower spike to appear just below the incision. Other plants such as peace lilies (*Spathiphyllum wallisii*) will flower on other parts of the plant, so prune off the dying flower as it browns.

A large windowsill holding multiple plants including *Pilea peperomioides*, *Strelitzia*, *Sansevieria trifasciata* 'Laurentii', *Ficus benjamina* 'Exotica', *Optunia*, *Sarracenia* and *Zamioculcas zamiifolia*.

Keep it pot-bound

The older the plant, the less frequently you should repot it. More mature specimens will prefer to be pot-bound (despite what some sources say) and can sometimes be more susceptible to transplant shock-related issues such as wilting or a loss of leaves.

Does my plant need a bigger pot?

A plant's pot size is a crucial element to its success. Houseplant root systems rarely like to be swimming in overly big pots with an ocean of soil. Instead, they like to be kept more pot-bound, until the time comes for a transplant.

SIGNS YOU NEED TO UPSIZE THE POT

— More than five roots escaping through the pot's bottom drainage holes. (One or two don't necessarily indicate a repot is needed.)
— The plant needs watering more often and has rapidly drying soil. (Remember: The more roots, the more likely each root-strand will fight over the moisture.)
— Some houseplants may exhibit a slowed growth rate.
— The plant's original soil feels brick-like (hardened) and doesn't absorb water quickly.

Plant-specific symptoms

— Monsteras and some other trailing plants may grow more aerial roots along their stem to compensate for the tight root system.
— Some houseplants such as ZZ plant (*Zamioculcas zamiifolia*) or mother-in-law's tongue (*Sansevieria trifasciata Laurentii*) have a strong root system that will dent or cause a bulge to appear in the pot's side. Plants that do this are better off being grown in a terracotta bulb planter, which can be found at garden centres in the outdoor pot section.
— Some flowering plants such as orchids and peace lilies (*Spathiphyllum wallisii*) may flower more often when pot-bound. In cases like this, repotting isn't always necessary if you're interested in promoting more blooms.

DO I ALWAYS NEED A BIGGER POT?

In around 90 per cent of cases, yes. It's good to give the plant a larger-sized pot to enable the root system to continue its ability to support an ever-growing specimen. The only times that you'll need a smaller pot is when a plant has severe root rot and needs to be downsized to restart the root system or you are dividing a plant into smaller plantlets. (See page 68 to learn more if you're worried about a dying rootball.)

A *Monstera deliciosa* in a pink ceramic pot accompanied by a *Clivia* in a gold metallic pot in a hallway.

Take your time

Never, ever rush repotting a plant. If you're too heavy-handed when you handle its roots (by pulling soil from healthy roots, or repotting while the soil is dry), your plant may develop 'transplant shock' (see page 74). A plant is always better being pot-bound than having its root system overly disturbed, so take the time to prepare!

HOW BIG A POT DO I NEED?

The general rule of thumb is to move your plant into a pot that's only a few centimetres (or a couple of inches) wider and deeper than its current one. If you're someone who's used to plastic pots, they'll come in uniform size intervals of volume (1 litre, 2L, 3L, etc., or the gallon equivalent for imperial) or diameter/width (5cm, 7.5cm, 9cm, 12cm, 15cm, 18cm, 20cm, 25cm, 30cm, 36cm, etc., or the inch equivalent). You need to work out your pot's current size by reading the number on the base (underneath) or by measuring the diameter of the pot from one end to another in centimetres or inches.

CAN I GIVE MY PLANT MORE ROOM IN ITS CURRENT POT?

There are times when you might not want to repot a plant into a larger pot – mostly, when you love the container it's in. You can still provide some new space to the rootball, despite the pot already being full of roots, by applying the 'top down' method:

1   Remove the top fifth of the soil before removing the whole plant from the pot. Try not to touch the roots or remove any compost from them.

2   Fill your now-empty pot one-fifth in depth with a fresh batch of potting mix (see page 66 for the correct mix).

3   Sit the rootball back in the part-filled pot and add soil to fill any remaining gaps.

4   Finally, apply a thin layer of fresh potting mix over the rootball.

5   Continue watering and feeding as normal.

This trick can be used on all healthy plants in any size of pot. Repotting in this way will give a plant around another year's worth of growth before you should consider a larger pot.

Top: A large *Strelitzia* plant makes a statement.

Bottom left: Three *Senecio rowleyanus* plants and a pot of seedlings benefit from a windowsill setting.

Bottom right: A wooden table is home to a *Ctenanthe burle-marxii* and a variegated Monstera.

Do plants need separate pots?

A question I get asked often is: Can I put these two plants together in the same pot? We are used to seeing plants grown in separate pots when visiting garden centres or nurseries, but is there a reason why they're almost always alone?

WHY DO I ONLY SEE PLANTS IN SEPARATE POTS?

There's a very simple reason why. Most houseplants are cultivated by division, seeds, stem cuttings or even tissue culture, and while young, they can be susceptible to disease. Especially when grown in the thousands, keeping each specimen apart makes it easy to sift out any dead or dying plants, all while localizing virus or bacteria spread to the singular pot. Furthermore, growing plants separately in pots is the quickest and most effective way to grow, distribute and sell houseplants across the globe, all while meeting each garden centre's different volume demands.

Three benefits of merging plants into one pot

1 More plants in less pots means you'll have more space in the home.

2 If you choose plants with different leaf textures, colours and sizes, you'll create a beautiful display to wow any guests who visit.

3 Growing plants within the same pot can provide mutual benefit to each plant. Some that I found hard to grow alone began to explode with new, healthy growth once placed in the same pot with others.

The best pot to grow the plants together is a terracotta bulb planter, which is available at all garden centres. Choose a planter that's deep enough to accommodate the total height of your plants' current pot (the one that it was purchased in).

As time goes on and the roots fill the pot, you may need to water and feed the soil more. This is a normal part of plant combination and is a great sign of health.

Are there any drawbacks?

The only difficulty is if you later want to separate the plants; the root systems will most likely be intertwined, so it is tricky to do so without causing transplant shock.

Interplay plants

Plants that need the same soil conditions, such as cacti and succulents, can be grown together, but try not to combine them with tropical/leafy plants such as monsteras, peace lilies (*Spathiphyllum wallisii*) or ferns. Tropical houseplants are best grown together in a 'houseplant'-labelled potting mix.

The bowl on the table contains *Portulacaria*, plus *Kalanchoe laciniata* and some green echeverias or sempervivums. Beside it on a pile of books is a bowl of *Haworthia limifolia*.

How do I propagate my plants?

A rack of test tubes filled three-quarters full with water to help a selection of tropical cuttings to root.

Propagating is a fantastic way to double your stock of a certain plant, as well as ensuring its legacy should it die suddenly from a pest or disease. Taking cuttings of older plants that have a sentimental value will enable you to grow carbon copies around your home.

There are a few crucial rules to follow with propagation, especially in the hygiene department. As you're opening up a big wound on both the mother plant and the new plantlet, there is a surface area that will be susceptible to bacterial rot. Here are some tips to prevent this:

The wound must be damage-free and 'simple'. Ensure that the wound is one continual cut, and not jagged, ripped or split. Think of a cucumber slice – it should be perfectly straight along the cut.

Clean your utensils and make sure they're sharp. Scissors, knives and secateurs should be clean and sharp before use. To clean them, just wipe the blades using either isopropyl alcohol (70 per cent or higher) or bleach (1 part bleach to 9 parts water). Always follow the manufacturer's safety recommendations.

Make sure you clean the utensils after each plant you work on, especially if the plant has pests or a disease.

For water propagation, ensure the water is replaced twice a week and that little to no leaves are submerged, as they may rot. Also, try pruning off any dying leaves, and remove whole stems if they become black and mushy, too.

Never use recycled water from other plants. Only fresh water (from the tap or bottle) is suitable.

More time in water

In some cases, newly potted cuttings may wilt after watering due to insufficient root maturity. Remove them from the soil, gently rinse to remove any soil, and cultivate in water until the roots are a little longer.

STEM CUTTINGS

Stem cuttings can be performed on most houseplants that have a physical stem. It's best to propagate once the plant is at least 12 months old (from when you bought it): remember that the older the plant, the better the stem cutting. Why, you may ask? Well, it's because of two things: the maturity of the stem and the overall length, which will increase the likelihood of rooting due to the higher number of nodes (point of growth for leaves and, more crucially, for potential roots). The general method of taking a cutting will be more or less the same for each plant, but a decision must be made if you're going to root it in soil or water. I prefer the latter, as I can see the progression a cutting will make when rooting in water; but propagating via soil is just as easy if you learn a few certain tricks, as mentioned below.

Taking a cutting

The perfect-sized cutting for vines such as *Monstera*, devil's ivy (*Epipremnum aureum*) or *Syngonium* is one that has two or three leaves. Each leaf will also have a node close by on the stem, which is where the roots will develop from in due course. Although you can propagate cuttings with less or more than the three leaves I recommend here, I find it easier to know how far into the soil to submerge the cutting's stems. The best area to take a cutting is at the very tip of each vine (where the new growth emerges), but don't be afraid to take more than one cutting off each vine if it's rather long. Just ensure you follow the two-or-three-leaf rule for each one.

For taking stem cuttings on wooded plants such as *Dracaena* or *Yucca*, I recommend taking cuttings by pruning the very top of a healthy stem. In terms of the size, think of a pencil length for the stem's length. Cuttings that have a stem around 15–20cm (6–8in) in length are best for quick rooting times, so don't prune too little off the mother/original plant.

Top left: Cuttings from a *Tradescantia*.

Top right: *Tradescantia* cuttings in water.

Bottom left: A *Ficus elastica* cutting in a glass of water with several small roots growing.

Bottom right: Healthy roots emerging from a *Ficus elastica* cutting.

Root rot rescue

It's good to note that taking cuttings this way is also a fantastic way to 'save' *Dracaena* or *Yucca* from severe root rot, where the plant is continuing to wilt. If the root system has died, no moisture will be transported from the soil and into the leaves, so propagating the stem will reconnect it to a water source when placed in a jar of water to root.

Tricky customers

Some houseplants can be a little tricky to root when propagating in water or soil. For plants within the *Ficus* family (fiddle leaf figs, weeping figs, etc.) or *Aralia* (fatsias, umbrella trees, etc.), I'd recommend dipping the bottom one-fifth of the cutting (the wound end) in rooting gel to speed up the growth rate. You'll want to apply the gel a few moments after pruning it off the mother plant, shortly before planting it in the pot of soil.

Root in soil or sphagnum moss

In addition to soil, you can also root cuttings in sphagnum moss, which is readily available at most garden centres. I sometimes propagate harder-to-root houseplants such as *Ficus* and umbrella trees (*Aralia*) in this medium, as the moisture from the moss creates a pocket of humidity around the plant, increasing rooting times.

1   Fill a 7cm (2¾in) pot with compost. Avoid peat-free multipurpose soils or those that are designed for outdoor use as they will be too heavy for what we're doing here. A 'houseplant'-labelled or coconut coir-based potting mix should be fine.

2   Arrange up to five cuttings around the edge of the pot. Place them half-deep into the soil, without any leaves physically being submerged under the soil. It's also important not to allow each cutting's foliage to rest on each other, as they'll need good air circulation to root.

3   Wrap the cuttings (and their pot) in a transparent bag or box with enough holes to promote air circulation. Don't let the bag or box touch the foliage; it should be large enough to accommodate the plant comfortably.

4   Ensure the soil is kept moist at all times by misting until the top 25 per cent is saturated. Remove any dropped leaves that lie on the soil or fully dead cuttings, to avoid disease.

5   You can remove the pot of cuttings from the bag or box once they produce their second leaf (while rooting). At this point, there will be a sufficient root system to power the plant in your home environment. Choose between keeping the cuttings together and only repotting next spring, or separating the cuttings and placing them in their own 7cm (2¾in) pot. It's your choice!

Treat the plant like a mature specimen by watering only once the top third of the soil dries out. Feed every third water and repot as necessary.

Root in water

I prefer to root tropical houseplant cuttings in water as it's easier to monitor them.

1   Place the cutting in a glass (or clear plastic) container just wide and deep enough to accommodate the bottom third of the plant's height and width.

2   Fill the container with water so that the bottom third of the plant is submerged. Keep the leaves out of the water to reduce the risk of leaf rot.

3   As the cutting is in a container of water, the reservoir should provide a sufficient level of humidity around the plant, so you won't need to do anything except refrain from placing the cuttings in full sun or near to an operating radiator.

4   Once the root system is sufficient, it can be transferred to a pot. A 'sufficient' and ready cutting can vary from plant to plant, but generally the roots must be at least 4cm (1½in) in length to support the cutting with moisture uptake from the newly potted soil.

5   Place the plantlet in a pot of 'houseplant'- labelled compost that's around a quarter of the cutting's size in height and has at least one drainage hole. Make sure the rootball is fully submerged in the soil. Place on a sunless windowsill for the optimum growth rate. Hydrate with a watering can and feed every third drink.

Take care

Successful propagation of cacti and succulents is mostly about dehydration. The 'body' parts of a succulent can be brittle and often snap at the slightest of touches, which is an evolutionary behaviour in order to survive in climates where rainfall is minimal. These fallen stems or leaves will root quickly in dry conditions, as they'll immediately search for moisture in the soil they have fallen on. This is why I recommend propagating succulent cuttings in dry soil and with minimal watering, to kick-start their root system.

LEAF CUTTINGS

Leaf cuttings are a fantastic way to propagate plants with multiple plantlets at once. Most of the time, cactus/succulent cuttings need soil as they require dry conditions to root. Tropical cuttings need moisture because their thin, generally larger, foliage loses moisture more quickly.

Streptocarpus and begonias

Due to hormones in the leaves, a streptocarpus or begonia can root from slits made across a leaf placed on top of a bed of moist soil.

1 Place a leaf cutting in a glass jar tall enough to hold half its overall height. Use a transparent container as it's important to see the root's progress and to know when the water is running low.

2 Take a seed tray (or a shallow, but wide container with drainage holes) and fill it three-quarters with 'houseplant'-labelled soil.

3 Place the cut leaf over the moist soil (not submerged) and hold it down, using pins, to make contact with the soil.

4 Place the tray in a transparent bag or box on a bright, indirect-sun windowsill.

5 Once small offsets grow from the slits and produce three leaves, you can grow them in their own 5cm (2in) pots.

Jade trees and Christmas cacti

Leaves that are halfway along the stem have the most potential for propagation due to their size and maturity.

1 Place your fingers between the mother's stem and the leaf's base, pulling it downwards until you hear a snap. Ensure the wound is intact with no damage – a bruise or tear will result in unsuccessful propagation.

2 Set the leaf on top of a bed of moist 'cactus and succulent'-labelled compost for root growth. Not only will this callous the wound (to prevent disease), but it will also speed up the propagation process considerably.

3 Once there is at least 3mm of root development, place the leaf one-third into the compost, at a slight diagonal angle. Provide a bright setting with temperatures around 18°C (64°F), with the majority of the soil drying out in between waters. New leaves should emerge within the next month.

A selection of begonia leaves await propagation.

RHIZOME CUTTINGS

Rhizomes are modified stems that grow horizontally across the soil (instead of upright) and are the base for the plant's above-soil foliage. They'll support the plant's leaves and even the root system, which means the central hub of the plant can be found here. You can take rhizomatous cuttings (essentially root cuttings) to split smaller divisions into separate pots. Only plants that have rhizomes can be propagated like this and each cutting must have at least one leaf attached to succeed; so it's important to only propagate a mature plant that has a large enough rhizome system to divide. Plants such as indoor bamboos, aspidistras and snake plants can be split this way.

Mother-in-law's tongue

This plant (*Sansevieria trifasciata Laurentii*) gets its name from its pointed leaves, which were said to symbolise a mother-in-law's sharp tongue. For this method, it's best to divide in the spring or summer and use offshoots at least half the mother plant's length of the blade.

Powering growth

This form of propagation is easier than you may think. Most rhizomes are relatively thick, so they store large amounts of moisture and nutrients. These will power the cutting's growth and significantly reduce the number-one risk of failed propagation - dehydration.

1   Take the plant out of its pot and place your hand in between the two growths; soil may have to be removed to get a better grip. Place your fingers around the nodal junction and gently push the offset downwards while supporting the mother plant.

2   Once it snaps, cautiously separate the two roots systems, keeping the roots intact and damage-free. Place the new plantlet in a 'Cactus & Succulent'-labelled soil and maintain the same care routines. If the offset doesn't have any roots, keep the compost on the dry side and they'll soon develop.

3   Never use a pot that is too big as a ratio of roots-soil that leans towards the latter will cause root rot. For the first couple of months, allow all of the soil to dry out in between waters and provide a bright, indirect setting for best growth.

4   Mother-in-law's tongues are best grown in terracotta 'bulb planters' which are typically shallow but wide in diameter. This pot shape will enable your plant's rhizomes to grow and fill the pot more effectively than typical upright pots.

Top: A *Pilea peperomioides* offset, often called a 'pup', is removed from a bare root system.

Centre: Two *Pilea peperomioides* 'pups' ready for repotting.

Bottom: A *Pilea peperomioides* 'pup' being placed in a pot of soil.

DIVISION

For plants such as prayer plants, Chinese evergreens, dumb canes (*Dieffenbachia*) and peace lilies (*Spathiphyllum wallisii*), you can also split the whole rootball into two (or even three) sections by teasing the separate plants apart. Similarly to prayer plants, you can tease other plantlets apart such as the nerve plant (*Fittonia*), and the polka dot plant (*Hypoestes*).

1 While being gentle with the root ball, tease the individual plant's root systems apart and remember to avoid unnecessarily pulling soil from the roots when they are already split

2 Repot the separated plants into smaller pots that are just big enough to accommodate the width of the rootballs.

3 Keep the soil moist and feed as necessary.

Five plants to grow from seed

Although a rare practice among indoor gardeners, there are certain houseplants that can be grown purely by seed. Of course, those little herb kits you probably received as a Christmas gift technically count as houseplants, but I'm talking more about the ornamental foliage plants like *Monstera*. Certain species of tropical or leafy houseplants make great seed projects when germinating at home, so let's look at a few examples.

Cheese plant (*Monstera deliciosa*)

Although commonly grown from stem cuttings, growing cheese plants from seed is much more fun. Why? Because their growth rate is prolific when they're young, so you can expect a specimen with multiple leaves within the first nine months from germination! The seeds can be purchased online.

Bird of paradise (*Strelitzia reginae*)

I always recommend beginners try bird of paradise seeds, as the seedlings are drought tolerant (to a degree). The only downside is that it will take a few years to have a specimen that's 30cm (1ft) in size, and up to eight years before it will produce a flower. The positive side to this is that due to the long lifespan of these plants (over 30 years in many cases), you'll create a living heirloom.

Orange spider plants
(*Chlorophytum orchidastrum*)

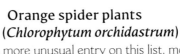

A more unusual entry on this list, most orange spider plants will produce a flower spike (and subsequent seeds) within one year of ownership. Wait for their seedpods to become brown and crispy before harvesting the small poppy-like seeds. Germination rates are rapid, with mine only taking ten days before leaves begin to emerge. So, when you buy one, you're actually buying multiple future plants, too.

Nerve plant (*Fittonia*)

As they are members of the mint family, it's no surprise that these plants germinate very quickly when exposed to soil. Within just two to three weeks, you'll see small seedlings emerge from the potting mix, and by the third leaf, their famous bright variegations will begin to show. These are perfect plants to get kids into growing, or for those who want to fill their home with unusually-coloured foliage in a short period of time.

Asparagus ferns
(*Asparagus setaceus*)

One of my true favourites, the asparagus fern makes for a fantastic houseplant due to its delicate leaves, which resemble miniature pine forests. The seeds are small with these plants and germination rates are around two weeks.

Five more plants

– Herbs such as coriander, chives, dill, mint and parsley
– Polka dot plant (*Hypoestes*)
– Coffee plant (*Coffea arabica*)
– Ponytail palm (*Beaucarnea recurvata*)
– Venus fly trap (*Dionaea muscipula*)

Styling
Your Plants

There are many ways people grow greenery indoors. Some people pass houseplants down through the generations as a 'living' heirloom; others grow a few herbs on the kitchen windowsill to spruce up their meals. You can use the leaf colour, shape and size of a plant to match the mood of a room.

Which plants will suit my decor?

Adding some greenery to your house will instantly make it a home. Plants make a place look lived in, along with softening the typical 90-degree angles of TVs, walls, furniture and floors. Although any plant will look good in any place, here are some matches that will help you achieve your desired aesthetic.

Vintage

Rubber plant
   (*Ficus elastica*)
Chinese money plant
   (*Pilea peperomioides*)
Mother-in-law's tongue
   (*Sansevieria trifasciata*
   'Laurentii')
Bird-of-paradise
   (*Strelitzia*)

Scandinavian

Asparagus fern (*Asparagus setaceus*)
Monstera

Plants create atmosphere

When selecting the plants, think about how they will complement the mood of a room. Does your home have a natural, dark or colourful look? Scandinavian homes tend to have natural brown, grey and cream; country homes usually sport deep red, blue, brown and gold.

Rustic

Yucca

Boston ferns
(*Nephrolepis exaltata*)

Weeping fig
(*Ficus benjamina*
'Exotica')

Cactus

Industrial

Blue star fern
(*Phlebodium aureum*)

Fishbone cactus
(*Epiphyllum anguliger*)

Minimalist
Bird of paradise (*Strelitzia*)

Five plants for maximum impact

A plant that has 'maximum impact' could be one that has bold, bright colours, such as a croton, beautiful flowers such as an orchid, or large, elephant-eared leaves such as a bird of paradise. I'll share some of the best options that will make a home immediately more welcoming, just by adding one or two plants.

Bonsai (*Ficus retusa*)

The first on my list may sound scarily difficult to grow, but if you have a large window (or bay window) that points north, east or west, why not try a bonsai-formed *Ficus retusa*? When correctly placed in sufficient lighting with partial sun, this plant is surprisingly easy to grow. Its 'S'-shaped trunk silhouetted against a window makes for a stunning cherry-topper in any bright room.

Black-gold philodendron (*Philodendron melanochrysum*)

The leaves of this plant are stunning at all angles. This species is best kept away from direct sunlight or operating radiators, so a table that's around 1m (3ft) from a window will suit it fine. The leaves have a dark-green shimmer, sliced by the lime-coloured veins that radiate from the centre.

Five more plants

- Vanda orchids
- Alocasia zebrina (*Alocasia zebrina*)
- *Caladium*
- False shamrock plant (*Oxalis triangularis*)
- False nerve plants (*Fittonia*)

Crotons (*Codiaeum variegatum*)

These vibrant houseplants can sport multiple-coloured leaves all at once. The brighter the location, the more vivid the foliage will look. I recommend keeping yours in either a north-west, north, or north-east facing window to provide the vital few hours of sunlight needed to entice its classic look. It's also good to note that a location that is too dark will force the croton to revert back to a fully-green appearance, so ensure yours receives partial sunlight for around two hours a day.

Ponytail Palm (*Beaucarnea recurvata*)

Chances are, if you're going to purchase a tall houseplant for a certain room of the house, you will see hundreds of options online or in store. Ponytail palms are ideal for sunny rooms, and ideally need overhead lighting from skylight windows as they struggle to thrive in small-windowed areas. For added visual interest, why not light up your palm at night? I do this and it absolutely transforms the aura in the room into a calm, relaxing one.

Moth orchids (*Phalaenopsis*)

One orchid is cute; two orchids are a pair; but three or more in a singular pot makes for a stunning display. Ensure yours receive enough light, so keep them within 1m (3ft) of a windowsill, with regular feeds of 'orchid'-labelled food. When bought all at the same time, your orchid display will flower for up to two months before the flowers slowly begin to drop off. Remember that even when the final bloom falls off one of the stems, you can easily entice it to re-bloom by pruning the stem back to a non-flowered node (see page 74).

How do I create a vined wall feature?

Epipremnum aureum in a terracotta pot starts to trail along a wall.

Training an indoor vine up a wall is both inexpensive and fun. No nails are required to achieve this, but be aware that the recommended adhesive hooks may leave small grease marks when removed. A vined houseplant growing along the wall of your home is as majestic as it is practical, and ideal if space is limited.

MAKING A VINED WALL

1 Stand with your back pressed against the wall, face the window(s) and use a compass to determine which way the window(s) face. If your room is south-east, south or south-west facing, you can opt for all varieties of philodendron or pothos. For rooms that point west, north or east, choose a variety that is mostly green.

2 Once you know the compass direction of your room, purchase a trailing plant recommended below. Choose the plant with the longest vines. Also, purchase some self-adhesive hooks as these will help to attach the vines to the wall.

3 Stand the plant against the wall (either on the floor for large plants with 70cm+ (28in+) vines, or on a piece of furniture for smaller specimens). Attach a self-adhesive hook to the tip of each vine and stick it to the wall, double checking the vine doesn't have much flex and is fully stretched out. Space each vine equally apart so the leaves from separate vines don't overlap. It's normal for a few leaves to yellow within a few weeks of being attached to the wall. Ensure the plant is well-fed with a 'houseplant'-labelled fertilizer and it'll bounce back with new growth in no time!

CHOOSING PLANTS FOR A VINED WALL
The four species below are easy to grow.

Heartleaf philodendron (*Philodendron hederaceum* 'Brasil')
The philodendron holds a fantastic divide of colours on its leaves. One half will enjoy the deep green typically found on many philodendrons, with the other being lavished in lime green, similar to the neon pothos.

Neon pothos (*Epipremnum aureum* 'Neon')
This eye-catching variety boasts a lime-coloured tinge to its foliage that will work in mid-century decor. It prefers bright locations and can even tolerate a few hours of morning or late-evening sunlight.

Propagation is key
After three years, your vined wall may look a little sparse near the soil as the oldest leaves die. This can be easily fixed by pruning the top 20cm (8in) off each vine every 18 months. Allow them to root in a jar of water and replant back into the mother's soil once the roots surpass 7cm (2¾in) in length!

Satin pothos (*Scindapsus pictus*)

Boasting a glaucous, blue-grey tone to its foliage, this species works well in farmhouse or industrial-style interiors. The leaves reliably hold a speckled variegation that glistens as you turn the leaf.

Snow queen pothos
(*Epipremnum aureum* 'Snow Queen')

This variety's light requirement can be tricky to ace at first, but as long as the plant is placed within 2m (6ft) of a window, it should be fine.

WHAT TO DO AS THE VINED WALL AGES (AND LOSES LEAVES)

Your vining houseplant may develop yellowing leaves from time to time, which is a natural part of its life. There are two perfectly good explanations for this, the first being its age. The most common symptom of maturity is yellowing or browning older leaves (closest to the soil), which may make your vined plant look a little bare at its base. The second explanation for the yellowing or loss of foliage is that the individual leaf that has died failed to collect enough light and, therefore, was sacrificed (to avoid predation in the wild). I have seen this with almost all pothos or philodendrons – whether they grow up, down or across a horizontal surface – so if you experience this, don't worry!

Regardless of which explanation applies to your wall, it is easily fixed. Take stem cuttings by pruning the top 12–20cm (5–8in) off the end of each vine with several leaves attached. Place the stems' bottom third (the end you've just cut) into water and wait until the roots are around 8cm (3in) in length. Place the rooted cuttings back into the mother plant's soil and soon you will have a bushy plant again.

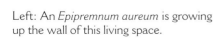

Left: An *Epipremnum aureum* is growing up the wall of this living space.

Right: A *Philodendron scandens* 'Brasil' vine.

How do I make an indoor thicket?

A thicket of plants grown in close proximity to create a community-like feel of foliage. Plants used here include Monstera, *Zamioculcas zamiifolia, Cycas revoluta, Sansevieria trifasciata* 'Laurentii', *Dracaena marginata, Livistona chinensis,* plus some cacti.

There are a lot of similarities between decorating a windowsill with houseplants and creating a thicket in the home. It's all about choosing plants with different pots, heights, leaf shapes and coloured foliage to create a display with dramatic contrast, as seen on page 108. But what is a thicket? The easiest answer is the 'grouping of plants in close proximity', and although it usually references outdoor greenery, the same principle can be applied indoors.

CHOOSING A LOCATION

As you can see in the images here, the best place to have an indoor thicket is by Juliet doors, in bay windows, or by large windows. Due to the close proximity within the group, each plant may fight for the light, so it's best to avoid arranging a thicket in shady corners (unless you use grow-light bulbs of more than 2,000 lumens). You can also make a thicket for a conservatory with sun-loving species.

IS THERE ANYTHING TO LOOK OUT FOR?

Choose plants with differing heights, leaf shapes and colours. You may have some plants looming around the home already, but if you're purchasing them from a shop, always check for pests (under the leaves and in the stems' cubbyholes) and any irrigation damage (such as root rot or excessive dehydration).

WINDOWS AND DOORS

Before heading down to your local garden centre, it is good to be aware of the window's/doors' light characteristics. A window (or room) that predominantly faces north-west, north, north-east or east will have minimal sunlight, so you can choose all tropical/leafy houseplants. For those that are pointing south-east, south and south-west, make sure you choose sun-tolerant plants.

A side table is home to *Cycas revoluta, Sansevieria cylindrica, Echeveria, Peperomia, Euphorbia, Howea forsteriana* and an *Aglaonema*.

A sunny corner is filled with a large palm, *Sansevieria trifasciata, Ficus lyrata, Philodendron, Monstera* and *Euphorbia trigona*.

Remember:
If the plant features in different lettered categories (A, B and/or C), you can purchase it in different sizes at the shop.

This thicket is home to contrasting leaf colours and shapes. Plants include a *Dracaena fragrans, Alocasia* 'Stingray', *Dypsis lutescens*, aloe and two *Syngonium*.

What plants are best to use?

It's important to use plants with differing heights. This list plots each plant's position categorized by size (A, B, C).

North
North-west, north and east-facing

A Large plants,
1m+ (3ft+) in height

Dracaena
Yucca
Pachira aquatica
Ficus elastica
Indoor cordylines
Aralia
Ficus 'Audrey'
Ficus lyrata
Sansevieria trifasciata

B Medium plants,
0.4–1m (1–3ft) in height

Dracaena
Yucca
Aralia
Epipremnum aureum, grown
   up a moss pole
Monstera
Ficus elastica
Ficus 'Audrey'
Ficus lyrata
Sansevieria trifasciata

C Small plants,
0.4m (1ft) in height

Epipremnum aureum
Zamioculcas zamiifolia
Chlorophytum comosum
Fittonia
Spathiphyllum wallisii
Nephrolepis exaltata
Indoor cordylines

South
South-east, south and south-west-facing

A Large plants,
1m+ (3ft+) in height

Yucca
Beaucarnea recurvata
Euphorbia trigona
Tall cacti
Sansevieria trifasciata
Crassula ovata

B Medium plants,
0.4–1m (1–3ft) in height

Yucca
Sansevieria trifasciata
Medium cacti
Crassula ovata

C Small plants,
0.4m (1ft) in height

Yucca
Zamioculcas zamiifolia
Chlorophytum comosum
Sansevieria trifasciata
Crassula ovata
Schlumbergera × buckleyi

Can I make my windowsill burst with foliage?

In regard to light levels, conditions found on a windowsill can be the closest to those of a houseplant's natural habitat. I experience the most joy when creating new displays bursting with different textures, colours and sizes, interplaying with indoor plants and pots. Although there is very little that can go wrong with mixing and matching, there are a few key tips worth knowing before you splash out on a new indoor oasis.

Check your window's compass direction

Being conscious of the angle at which the direct sunlight enters your room is the first step to consider. Those with south-east, south or south-west-facing windows are most likely to receive the brunt of the afternoon sun and, therefore, will require thicker-leaved plants or those that can store moisture in their roots, stems or leaves (cacti or succulents). North-west, north and north-east windows are much easier to interplay as the sunlight isn't too strong, even in the height of summer.

Check for pests and disease

Once you're happy with the chosen windowsill(s), it's time for the fun part: heading to your local plant shop or garden centre to see what's on offer. Always check for pests before bringing anything home, as this is the most common way to introduce an infestation into your plant collection. Plant parts to inspect are the stems, leaves, flowers and any other cubbyholes where a pest may lay an egg-mass (the fancy word for its HQ!). Some egg-masses may be small, cottony fluffs, as with mealybugs; others may look like small spiders' webs along the creases of leaves (spider mites). If there are any fungus gnats, don't worry too much as you can always replace the top layer of soil for a fresh batch, to remove the eggs or larvae entirely.

Protect wooden windowsills with coasters or saucers

Once you have chosen your plants based on colour, texture and personal preference, it is equally as important to ace the pot design. Some indoor gardeners like to have an all-terracotta display, whereas others like to combine metal, ceramics, clay or coir with their foliage. If the decorative pot you've picked out has drainage holes or is made of terracotta, place a saucer underneath so that any escaped water doesn't damage the windowsill. You can also repurpose lids from used food packaging, or use old chipped plates to save money and be eco-conscious.

Quick tips on aftercare

Caring for houseplants on the windowsill is arguably easier than in any other location in the home purely due to easy, hip-height access and the higher rates of photosynthesis that power them. You may need to water them a little more often than you would with plants further away from the window, but as long as you're mindful of drying soil, you'll find this easy.

A kitchen windowsill bursting with various sized houseplants, creating a curtain-like privacy wall with their foliage. Plants include: *Clivia, Pilea, Chlorophytum comosum, Strelitzia, Sansevieria trifasciata* 'Laurentii', *Echeveria, Ficus benjamina* 'Exotica', cactus, sarracenia, *Opuntia* and *Zamioculcas zamiifolia*.

A collection of cacti and succulents on a sunny windowsill, including *Haworthiopsis, Dracaena, Mammillaria* and a *Gymnocalycium mihanovichii.*

SUNNY AND/OR DARK

Due to the higher temperatures and exposure to the sun's UV rays in windows and conservatories facing south-east, south and south-west, choose plants that originate from arid or exposed locations such as deserts or rocky hillsides. Cacti, succulents, bulbs, carnivorous and fleshy species are the best options here. You can even create a desert-themed terrarium with dried bark and slate to further reinforce the theme.

DARK AND/OR COOL

Your creative flair can really rise to the surface in places that are dark and/or cool, such as windowsills facing north-east, north and north-west. Tropical plants are popular, so the variety available is second to none. You can create a display based on a colour scheme (purple foliage, decorative pots, etc.) or use the power of contrast to achieve a magnificent display. Most houseplants, including succulents, can be used in north-facing windows.

Tropical plants on a wooden windowsill with partial sunlight include a calathea, *Alocasia* and a philodendron.

How do I make a hanging basket?

Indoor hanging baskets are similar to garden ones – but there are more plants to choose from.

Most hanging baskets are made of pressed coir, where the excess moisture drains out of the bottom when watered. As you obviously don't want this to happen in your home, choose a wide, shallow, decorative ceramic pot with no drainage holes. If you're worried about the weight of the display, look for a woven basket with a plastic lining.

1 Use a pot that will fit your plants. I prefer one that's at least 14cm (5½in) deep so I can use small houseplants that grow in 12cm (4¾in) plastic pots. Alternatively, use a smaller pot and plants, but remember: the smaller the plant, the quicker it will dry out and need watering.

2 Use houseplants that will sit in the container without their individual plastic pot being too visible. Choose plants that have contrasting colours and textures. You can mix in flowering plants including bromeliads and orchids, and pendulous ones such as spider plants (*Chlorophytum comosum*) and neon pothos will look fabulous hanging over the edge.

3 Due to the lack of drainage holes, don't put your plants directly into the decorative pot. Instead, keep them in their plastic pots and sit them inside the decorative one.

4 Purchase (or make) a macramé braid that fits your pot. Make sure the rope isn't too tight to leave space for the plants to grow. Once you're happy with the pot and holder, hang the display from a hook (in the wall or ceiling) to bring it to life.

The branch of a tree holds macramé pot holders and plants including *Sansevieria trifasciata* 'Laurentii' and *Epipremnum aureum*.

Aftercare

You'll need to hydrate the plants from time to time. Water the soil like I mention on page 38. Feed every third water for tropical/leafy and flowering houseplants, except for cacti and succulents, which will only need fertilizing every three months.

Wall-mounted half-baskets are a great addition to a home, especially those with minimal space. Just make sure you purchase ones without drainage holes and ensure they never become waterlogged after hydrating the plant inside.

CHOOSING THE BEST HOUSEPLANTS FOR HANGING BASKETS

Growing multiple species together in the same pot is highly beneficial for each plant, but you must consider its location and, more precisely, the light levels. There are two things to remember about an indoor hanging display. Firstly, never place it more than 2m (6ft) away from a light window, unless it's in a room with a skylight. Secondly, choose the right plants – you don't want to place a shade-loving fern in a hot conservatory; likewise, a desert-themed display won't thrive in a shady spot. I've listed two areas in the home and the most suitable plant options for each setting below.

Plants for hot conservatories

Due to health and safety risks, try not to use sharp cacti in these displays. Instead, for a desert-themed display that is also drought tolerant – so you won't need to be watered as often – try using upright succulents such as aloes, jade trees (*Crassula ovata*), sansevierias and haworthias. They can be mixed with trailing succulents that will hang over the pot, such as *Rhipsalis*.

Plants for shaded conservatories

For bright locations that don't offer any or much sunlight, you can choose most tropical/leafy houseplants. Here are a few suggestions based on easy, non-fussy care requirements. If you want upright/tall plants, try parlour palms (*Chamaedorea elegans*), dumb canes (*Dieffenbachia*), dragon trees (*Dracaenas*), crotons and bush lilies (*Clivia*). Prayer plants and mosaic plants (*Fittonia*) can be challenging when grown at height, as you can't always check the soil moisture for an indication of when to water again.

Plants to trail over the edge of a pot

These examples look great when allowed to grow over the edge of the pot:
– Spider plant (*Chlorophytum comosum*)
– Devil's ivy (*Epipremnum aureum*)
– Heartleaf philodendr*ons (Philodendron hederaceum 'Brasil')*
– Swedish ivy (*Plectranthus verticillatus*)
– *Tradescantia*
– *Rhipsalis*

Flowering plants for hanging baskets

Add a splash of colour with:
– Orchids
– *Schlumbergera × buckleyi* (they also have trailing leaves)
– Bromeliads (*Vriesea, Bromelia* and *Neoregelia*)
Avoid short-lived flowers such as flaming Katie, or challenging plants such as flamingo flowers (*Anthurium andraeanum*).

Top: Wall vases hold *Rhipsalis*, hoyas and *Nephrolepis exaltata*.

Bottom left: A hoya is suspended in front of a bright window.

Bottom right: A *Senecio rowleyanus* and *Haworthiopsis* combine in this window display.

How do I make a plant bowl?

A plant bowl is a decorative pot filled with a display of houseplants that live together happily. There are two plant groups you can use: tropical or desert dwellers. Never mix them in the same display.

Five quick tips before you get started

Choose a wide, shallow pot with a drainage hole in the base; I recommend terracotta bulb planter pots. Make sure it is only 5cm (2in) deeper than the tallest pot your plants are currently in.

- Use plants you already own, or choose ones with contrasting colours. Check for pests and root rot before placing the plants together. If in doubt, have a look on page 132 to identify a pest.

- Choose the right soil mix. Tropical displays must be planted in 'houseplant'-labelled compost, whereas desert dwellers are best grown in 'cactus and succulent'-labelled potting mixes.

- Put the tall plants at the back of the pot and smaller ones at the front.

PLANTS FOR TROPICAL DISPLAYS

The tall plants I recommend for these bowls are: purple-leaved cordylines, green-leaved parlour palms (*Chamaedorea elegans*), dragon trees (*Dracaena*) and peace lilies (*Spathiphyllum wallisii*).

   To cover the soil, choose nerve plants (*Fittonia*), devil's ivy (*Epipremnum aureum*), Swedish ivy (*Plectranthus verticillatus*) or *Pothos* which has green, lime-green, yellow, white or glauca leaves (depending on the variety). The green and white leaves of a medium-height spider plant (*Chlorophytum comosum*) will eventually trail with stolons (runners). The dark-green Christmas/Thanksgiving cacti (*Schlumbergera* × *buckleyi*) produces flowers in mid-to late autumn. They are tall, but can trail if planted near to the edge of the pot.

PLANTS FOR DESERT DISPLAYS

Cacti and succulents are ideal for desert displays. The tall plants
I suggest for plant bowls are the African milk bush (*Euphorbia trigona*)
and jade plants (money trees). For added visual appeal, look for
ponytail palms (*Beaucarnea recurvata*), *Cephalocereus senilis*, *Opuntia*
and any species of *Sansevieria*. Arrange these with plants that grow
into ball shapes. Try *Echinocactus*, *Gasteria*, aloes, haworthia or the
ladyfinger cactus (*Mammillaria elongata*).

Several succulent species, including a *Haworthiopsis*, *Opuntia*, aloe and an *Adromischus*, share a bowl.

How do I underplant a large plant?

'Underplanting' is where you plant a smaller houseplant within a larger plant's soil, to either create a contrast of foliage colour or to 'bush' (fill) out the plant. Combining two or more together will benefit all the plants involved, and can eventually save you space, so you can buy even more plants!

WHICH PLANTS CAN I UNDERPLANT WITH?

As with making a terrarium (see page 122), you must choose plants that enjoy the same soil conditions and light levels. Most tropical/leafy houseplants will work well together, but check for pests on the newly bought plant to avoid any spreading. Have a look under the foliage and around the cubbyholes of stems for critters such as spider mites, thrips and scale.

You can merge any of the following together: calatheas, Chinese evergreens (*Aglaonema*), devil's ivy (*Epipremnum aureum*), *Sansevierias*, *Ficus*, *Pachiras*, palms, peace lilies (*Spathiphyllum wallisii*) and umbrella trees (*Aralia*).

To get around succulents such as aeoniums, aloes, *Echeveria* and jade trees (*Crassula ovata*) becoming leggy after a few years, snip the stems for cuttings and directly plant back into the soil to improve overall appearance.

Do I have to use a different species of plant?

Not at all! In some cases, your houseplant may become leggy after a while; let's take a monstera, for example. After a few years, the old leaves will yellow and drop off, with new growth emerging solely from the top. This means the bottom area of the plant (above the soil) becomes bare. In cases like this, you could underplant smaller cheese plants (*Monstera deliciosa*) in the soil to thicken the overall foliage.

Dypsis lutescens and an anthurium that's currently in bloom create a stylish arrangement.

SO, HOW DO I UNDERPLANT?

In the host plant's soil, create a hole deep enough to slot in the smaller plant's rootball. Be cautious of damaging the host's roots, so only dig between a quarter to a third the depth of its pot. If the smaller plant is too big, take some cuttings from it and root those in water before planting into the host's soil (see page 85).

The plant that works anywhere

The ultimate plant that will work well with ALL tropical/leafy houseplants is the trusted neon pothos (*Epipremnum aureum* 'Neon'). You can easily insert both pot-bought specimens or individual cuttings into the soil and it will immediately green-up the brown soil below. They're not difficult to grow, either, so don't worry if you forget to hydrate the soil. Another example is the nerve plant (*Fittonia albivenis*), which comes in different red, yellow and orange tones, but it tends to be more delicate when it comes to watering regimes, so I would stick with pothos.

Window light

Only underplant a host plant if its soil has a clear visual line towards the window. If there's furniture in the way that blocks the light hitting its soil, don't underplant.

How do I make a terrarium?

Left: A finished sealed terrarium comprising a *Ficus benjamina* and a *Fittonia*.

Centre: A collection of six terraria.

Right: Handle plants sich as these succulents with care when arranging them in a terrarium.

Creating a terrarium is fun for all the family. From picking a couple of cute plants at your local garden centre to building it from scratch, it's a great way to escape from daily stress and focus on a calming task.

I started my business selling desert-themed terraria online. Once a week I delivered them to people living nearby. I also started to collect terraria containing different species of woodlice and millipedes – creatures I found fascinating as a kid. I loved creating biomes where I could feed and nurture them, and watch as they doubled in number in a year or so. Within minutes of placing a banana peel on the terrarium floor, it was covered in woodlice taking a bite to eat!

A collection of desert-based terraria with various cacti, aloes and an *Echeveria*.

The method of planting up a terrarium is the same whatever theme you chose. Here is my step-by-step guide to doing it.

1   Pour around 4–5cm (1½–2in) of the stones into your empty terrarium and level them off. You can use 0–2cm (0–0.8in) of pebble-like aquarium stones, or 'horticultural grit'. If you're making a jungle-themed display (see page 126), pour a thin layer 1mm (0.04in) of activated charcoal over them.

2   For jungle displays: Mix 3 parts 'terrarium'-labelled soil to 1 part worm castings. If you don't want to use this, or are making a desert-themed display, skip this step.

3   Pour 4–5cm (1½–2in) of soil mix on top and level it. From a bird's eye view, mark which half of the terrarium will be the back, and which half will be the front. The aim is to have the tall plants towards the back, so the front is left unobstructed for the smaller plants, decorative rocks and mini figures.

4 Take any tall or large plants out of their plastic pots and gently loosen the rootball. Rather than removing soil from the roots, break up the rootball's overall shape. Sit the plants on top of the soil in the back area.

5 Next, remove your smaller plants from their pots. Loosen the rootballs and sit them on the soil in the front of the terrarium.

6 Pour the remaining soil around the plants until it meets the tops of the rootballs. Water the plants (the watering method depends on the theme of the terrarium, see the relevant pages). Ensure the soil is level and has no sudden dips.

7 Add your decorations (larger stones, bark fragments, mini figures). This is the time to welcome any little critters to a jungle terrarium (see page 126). For a desert display, why not pour a 1cm (½ in) layer of sand over the soil to make it look even more arid.

JUNGLE THEME: LEAFY AND TROPICAL

What's the best container to use?

Create a closed terrarium for plants that like high humidity and reliable soil moisture. Although an open terrarium (one without a lid) is fine, you'll need to water the display often, so closed is more practical.

The container should be deep enough to accommodate at least 10cm (4in) of aggregate and a further 20cm (8in) for the foliage.

Which plants are best for a jungle terrarium?

Use upright plants for height: bromeliads (*Tillandsia, Billbergia, Bromelia* and *Vriesea)*; calatheas; crotons; Boston ferns (*Nephrolepis exaltata*); wood ferns (*Dryopteris*); maidenhair ferns (*Adiantum*); *Pilea mollis*; parlour palm (*Chamaedorea elegans*); *Pilea involucrata*; and syngoniums. My choice of ground-cover plants are: baby's tears (*Soleirolia soleirolii*); turtle vines (*Callisia*); nerve plants (*Fittonia*); peat moss (*Sphagnum*); maidenhair vines (*Muehlenbeckia*); and spider wort (*Tradescantia*).

What should I use for drainage and decoration?

Use a 'terrarium'-labelled potting mix, two tall plants and three ground-cover plants, then add 2–6mm (0.08–0.2in) grit or stones and activated charcoal for drainage. I also include worm castings; these are optional, but will improve soil health. For decoration, try fragments of dried bark and larger stones (5cm+/2in+) – I prefer white stones as they give a nice contrast against the foliage and soil. Finally, pop in jungle, rainforest or explorer-based movie mini figures.

Any quick tips for caring for my new jungle terrarium?

The best location is a windowsill where direct sunlight is at a minimum, as the rays may scorch delicate leaves. If you have used an open container, keep the soil moist by pouring water slowly into the soil. Never allow the potting mix to become fully dry or waterlogged; instead, water a little and often. You may only need to pour around 50ml (1½fl oz) at a time. Check the side of the glass for a pool of water if you're worried about it being over-watered. If this happens, keep the room temperature warm and don't water until plants soak up the water in the pool. Shortly after making a closed terrarium, mist the inside (over the foliage and inside the glass) until the soil becomes damp. Don't water with a can or jug as you may pour in too much. For open terraria, fertilize every third water using a 'houseplant'-labelled feed. Closed displays won't need feeding as often.

A sealed terrarium of a *Ficus retusa* and a *Fittonia*, accompanied by moss and stones.

DESERT THEME: CACTI AND SUCCULENTS

What's the best container to use?

Due to their adaptation to dry and sunny habitats, cacti and succulents prefer to be out in the open. Choose a container with an opening at least 12cm (5in) in diameter, or a fully open bowl, to promote air circulation around the display and plants. Planting desert dwellers in an enclosed display with moist soil will increase the risk of them rotting.

Which plants are best for a desert terrarium?

Most plants within the cactus and succulent section of a plant shop will be suitable. The only species to avoid are tropical cacti, such as mistletoe (*Rhipsalis*) or Christmas cacti (*Schlumbergera* × *buckleyi*).

I recommend the following plants to add height: aeoniums, *Aloe vera*, crassulas, elephant's bush (*Portulacaria afra*), *Crassula ovata*, mother-in-law's tongue (*Sansevieria trifasciata* 'Laurentii'), pachypodiums, ponytail palms (*Beaucarnea recurvata*), bunny ear cacti (*Opuntia microdasys*) and saguaro cacti. The ideal shorter plants are: echevierias, gasterias, monk's hood cacti (*Astrophytum ornatum*), golden barrel cacti (*Echinocactus grusonii*), spider cacti (*Gymnocalycium baldianum*), haworthias, mammillarias, living stones (*Lithops*) and sedum.

Size matters

Choose plants grown in 5–10cm (2–4in) pots to avoid buying specimens too big for your display.

What should I use for drainage and decoration?

Use 'cactus and succulent'-labelled potting mix, and two tall plants and three smaller/shorter plants, then add 2–6mm (0.08–0.2in) grit or stones and activated charcoal for drainage (the charcoal is also a soil additive). To decorate the display, add sand on top of the soil once it is potted up to make it look like a desert, then add dried bark, slate or clay-coloured stones and create a mountain landscape using slightly larger stones (5cm+/2in+). For a finishing touch, include Wild West or desert-themed mini figures.

Any quick tips for caring for my new desert terrarium?

A sunny window is paramount for success. Even if it's only an hour or two per day, the warmth from the sun will help dry the soil out more quickly. The aim is to keep a desert terrarium dry most of the time. The best place is an east, south or west-facing window.

Water the base of each plant with a tablespoon or pipette. Don't drench the soil; instead, three tablespoons of water at the base of the plants is enough, usually once every three to four weeks. If in doubt, don't water. They will survive a while without a drink! Mix in 'houseplant'-labelled feed during a water twice a year – in spring and mid-summer.

Remove yellow or dying leaves and replace any dead plants.

Pests & Problems

Don't panic! If you catch a pest early, there is always time to assess, plan and eradicate it before the plant shows any signs of distress. As you'll discover, there are a number of simple and environmentally safe ways to identify and eradicate certain critters from your indoor oasis.

Help, I've seen a pest! What is it?

There are seven main characters in the world of houseplant pests. Some are harmless, others can cause considerable damage within a short timeframe. In this section, I'll mention all of them, ranging from the harmless to the most harmful for our beloved green friends.

Spider mites

There are five main stages in a spider mite's 30-day life. Due to their rapid reproduction rates, a single year can see up to 20 generations within one plant, all producing up to a hundred eggs per adult. They'll produce small, silvery webs that measure up to 1cm (½ in) in diameter along the stems, flowers and leaf creases. An adult is most likely to sport a light-yellow appearance and will be the size of a sand grain. Most houseplants are susceptible to spider mites, especially those with broad, thin leaves (ferns, monsteras, prayer plants and alocasias). The webs themselves aren't harmful to the plant, but there'll be hundreds of eggs within them that'll be ready to hatch and attack the nearby foliage.

Mealybugs

Few people know this, but the white oval critters that lounge around on a houseplant's leaf or stem are the females. They mostly remain stationary on a leaf or stem, providing food and protection for their offspring. Male mealybugs are winged and can fly up to 400m (0.2 miles) to look for mates, but they rarely damage houseplants as they can't 'eat'. Their lifespan can be up to three months, and a single critter can produce up to a hundred eggs. Common symptoms of a mealybug attack are yellowing and browning leaf-edges, sticky leaves, or white, cotton-like structures between the leaves, stems and flowers.

Soil mites and springtails

Both of these pests are entirely harmless to the plant. In fact, they'll complement the microbial activity and recycle nutrients back into the soil for the plant's overall benefit. Both bugs are less than 2mm (0.08in) in length and are often a shade of white, cream or grey. Springtails have a unique adaption to avoid hungry predators by jumping away to a distance up to 260 times their size with their 'furcula' (fork-like appendages that extend from under their bellies).

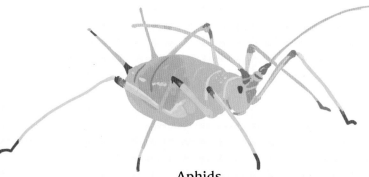

Aphids

Although it will take a while for damaged leaves to become noticeable, the reproductive rates of aphids are phenomenal. Within a few weeks, a single aphid can produce up to 50 offspring. What's more fascinating is that with some species, the female carries offspring that already have their own offspring inside, too, meaning that two future generations can be housed simultaneously. Due to their weak mouthparts, most infestations will only occur on the soft tissue of a plant, which includes the juvenile leaves, buds and flowers.

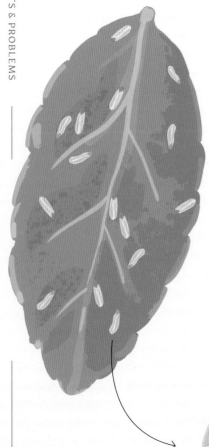

Scale

Most commonly found on umbrella (*Aralia*) and citrus trees, scale is one of the most difficult pests to remove in a single attempt. Due to their hard-armoured cover that stretches over the body, attempts should be made to physically pick off each critter as you see them. Most scales can reach up to 0.8mm (0.03in) in diameter and are often ovular or circular-shaped; some are brown, whereas others might be orange or golden in colour. A typical scale will live for around three months and can have up to three generations per year. In some species, the male has small wings to enable cross-breeding on nearby plants. Be mindful of a species called euonymus scale, which is white and oblong as opposed to circular and brown like most species of scale.

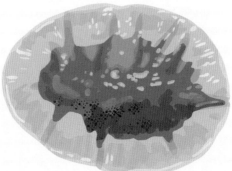

Helpful pests

Generally speaking, any 'pests' that you see in the soil are harmless to a plant. They help condition the soil by recycling the organic matter found in a potting mix and, in turn, promote microbial activity that the plant can benefit from. This is why some indoor gardeners choose to leave soil mites and springtails in their houseplant's compost.

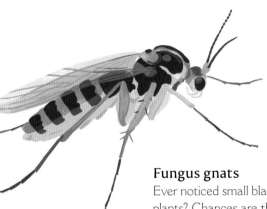

Fungus gnats

Ever noticed small black flies hovering around your home and indoor plants? Chances are they're fungus gnats, which eat, breath and sleep potting mix. With a single gnat living for only four weeks, their population can nonetheless appear to come from nowhere. A single gnat can produce up to two hundred eggs and will favour laying them in reliably moist (sometimes over-watered) soil. If you're wondering which plant(s) may be the culprit for housing these unwanted guests, check those that are grown more than 2m (6ft) away from a window and those on shelves or corners of the room. The eggs and larvae are white and measure up to 3mm (0.1in) in length, whereas the adult gnats are black and winged, and will be much easier to spot. It's good to note that both the adult fungus gnat and its eggs/larvae are completely harmless to the plant. They actually benefit the soil's overall health, so it's not a requirement to remove this bug if you come across it!

Thrips

The final pest on this list is by far the most damaging within a short period of time. When thrips are spotted on a plant, you must act swiftly to avoid them causing further damage to the affected plant and others nearby. Each critter will live for around a month and can lay up to two eggs a day – a hundred in total. Unlike mealybugs and scale, the male thrip looks almost identical to a female, albeit slightly smaller. The larvae (of any gender) are yellowish, whereas the mature adults become black within two weeks and can measure up to 1.5mm (0.06in) in length. Both are oblong-shaped.

How do I stop pests from spreading?

I've had my fair share of pests that have come and gone across my large plant collection and I've discovered that the art of preventing an infestation from spreading is simple. In this section, I'll guide you on some quick-fire tips to avoid giving a pest the opportunity to jump from plant to plant.

LIMITING SOIL-BORNE INSECTS (SOIL MITES, SPRINGTAILS, FUNGUS GNATS)

As repotting is a key step in removing bugs within the soil, make sure you don't reuse the old soil for another houseplant. Instead of discarding the compost, why not mix it into the garden or outdoor potted plants? The soil shouldn't be diseased, so it won't cause any detrimental effect to the outdoor ecology.

Whether or not you have repotted your plant, keep the affected specimen at least 1m (3ft) away from others. Ensure that the new location promotes a similar light level to the plant's original one to avoid 'environmental shock'.

If you repot a plant while it has issues of insects, the plant may become overly stressed and this could hinder its revival. That's why it's best to keep the plant snug in its original pot until the critters have been absent for at least three months. Fungus gnat larvae love moist soil in dark areas, so ensure your plant isn't watered too frequently. I'd recommend checking the pot's weight for soil moisture; only rehydrate when it feels light when lifted.

And finally, remember that soil-borne insects are entirely harmless to the plant, so don't panic when you first notice activity within the compost.

LIMITING LEAF PESTS
(ALL OTHER PESTS: MEALYBUGS,
SPIDER MITES, THRIPS)

An *Aeonium* in
a terracotta pot.

Regardless whether you have treated the plant for leaf pests, it's best
to quarantine them to avoid cross-contamination. Space affected
plants at least 1m (3ft) away from other plants, but preferably in a
separate room. If you don't have the room to arrange the plants like
this, try keeping the affected plant(s) in a transparent box with a lid
– drill holes in the lid to allow the air to circulate. It's also important to
ensure that the location has enough intensity of light to keep the plant
happy.

Prune away the most affected stems or leaves if the majority has
become yellowed or brown. Don't remove the leaf if it's still green
after removing any pests, though.

And finally, keep the plant well-fed. Follow a 'houseplant'-labelled
fertilizer's recommendation on strength and frequency to boost the
plant's overall strength and limit the damage caused by pests.
A stronger plant can usually tolerate pests more effectively.

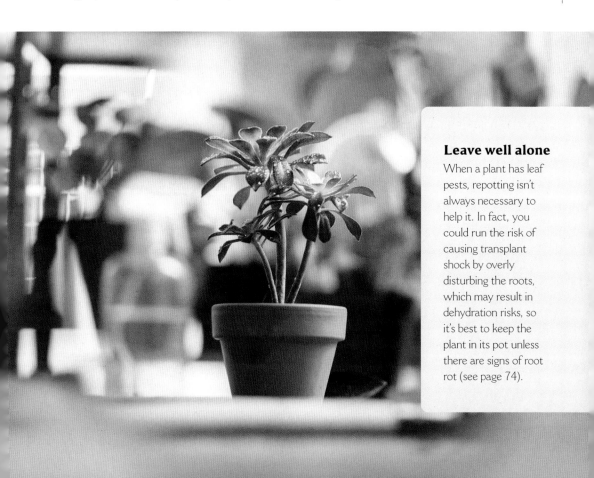

Leave well alone

When a plant has leaf
pests, repotting isn't
always necessary to
help it. In fact, you
could run the risk of
causing transplant
shock by overly
disturbing the roots,
which may result in
dehydration risks, so
it's best to keep the
plant in its pot unless
there are signs of root
rot (see page 74).

How do I sort out a leggy houseplant?

'What causes a plant to become leggy?' I hear you ask. Well, in most cases, it means you're doing a good job with its care requirements. Houseplants will age like trees and shrubs outside, continuing to grow at the tips of the stems with little new leaves being pushed out at the base (near the soil). The older leaves will eventually drop off as they reach the end of their life, so when a plant solely grows at the stem's tip, it'll become 'naked' at the bottom.

SO, HOW DO I PREVENT LEGGINESS?

Decapitation. It sounds like a drastic measure, but pruning the top of your plant will force the hormones and nutrients back down to the lower portions of the stem. This is what's known as removing its 'apical dominance', and will entice the plant to produce new branches in the bare areas.

1 In terms of *where* to prune, there are two factors to consider. The first is to learn how to spot a 'node', which is essentially a point of growth on a stem where a plant can produce an entirely new branch of leaves. On most plants, you'll want to prune around 2.5cm (1in) above a node to ensure bacteria, or the damage won't kill the chances of regrowth.

2 The second element to remember is to know *how much* of the stem you can safely remove. It's generally safe to reduce the plant's overall height by a third, but some can tolerate being cut closer to the soil (further down). But before you rush to slice down your green friends, some prefer their rootball to be split into several sections. Keep reading to learn about each category of plant.

Keep it light

If your plant is leggy and you purchased it within six months, you may be keeping it in a too-dark location. The plant is stretching towards the light and not growing in a steady way to support its balance. Move it closer to a window, or place the grow-light closer to its foliage.

A mature *Echeveria elegans* with leggy stems that spill over the sides of its pot.

Rhizomatous and tuberous plants
(Mother-in-law's tongue, prayer plants, cast-iron plants)
The stems of some houseplants are underground and grow horizontally under the soil. The best way to stop these plants from being leggy is to split the rootball by half or thirds. Ensure the soil is pre-moistened before taking the plant out of its pot, then split the rootball in half by teasing the roots. If they don't split easily, use a clean knife to cut the rootball in two. Repot into individual pots that fit the roots snug. Use a suitable potting mix and keep on a sunless windowsill for two months.

Succulents
(Jade trees, echeverias, string of pearls, flaming Katy)
If you've owned a succulent for several years, you'll find that it becomes tall, with bare, gangly stems. This is natural and a common behaviour for species that originate from low-rainfall habitats. Prune the stem back to a desired height (either a third down or halfway) and reduce the frequency of watering. As most (or all) of its leaves will be removed, the plant won't draw up moisture, so don't fall in the trap of over-watering – once every two weeks should be enough. You can propagate cuttings back in the mother plant's soil, or in a 9cm (3½in) pot of 'cacti'-labelled potting mix, to start a new plant from scratch.

Upright plants
(Yucca, dragon trees, French peanuts, umbrella trees, figs)
This group of plants are the most common and easy to prune due to their upright stem. Similarly to pruning a tree, you can either:

- Cut the main stem back by a third (if it's just growing a single vertical trunk). This will reduce the plant's overall height and promote more individual branches to pop up across the stem.
- If your plant is bushy already, snip each individual tip by 2.5cm (1in). Ensure each branch is pruned, otherwise the plant will prioritize growth on the non-pruned areas.

Vined/training plants
(Devil's ivy, lipstick plants, hoyas, string of pearls)
Especially when a plant cascades down a shelf or hanging pot, it will eventually look bare at the top (over the soil). Again, this is entirely natural and is the product of maturity as the plant ages. Reduce the stem's overall length by a third (or more) and propagate the prunings in water. Once their roots are around 5cm (2in), repot them back into the mother plant's soil to thicken the greenery. The original pruned stems should have also rebranched by this point, too.

A *Maranta leuconeura* showcasing its variegated foliage with red veins.

Keep it well-fed

Feeding is important for a plant to have enough energy to rebranch when being pruned. Ensure that your tropical/leafy plant is fertilized once every second or third water with a 'houseplant'-labelled feed both before and after the cutback. Cacti and succulents don't need feeding often, so try to nourish the soil only every three months. Never fertilize a carnivorous plant; instead, ensure it receives a few hours of sunlight per day to encourage regrowth after pruning.

Are my trailing houseplants happy?

Regardless of whether you grow a trailing plant on a shelf or hang it off something, there are some heads-ups to know about, to avoid killing it. Unless the plant is grown directly under a window or in a windowsill, treat it as a 'low light' area.

SPECIAL CARE

Growing plants at heights of more than 1m (3ft) from the ground will sit above the diagonal line of natural daylight that will illuminate any room.

Root rot is a common problem with plants on shady shelves, so, if there's one thing I hope you remember from this page, it's to not water the soil too frequently. Only rehydrate once the pot feels light when lifted; while the plant is heavy it won't need a drink. (Turn to page 25 to read my top five dos and don'ts with plant care in dark areas.)

LOSING LEAVES

It's perfectly normal for a plant to lose a few leaves within the first two to three months of being placed on a shelf, due to environment change. Looking further along the line, it's also fine if the plant begins to appear naked at the top (near to its soil) after a couple of years. This is purely old age, and can be remedied by snipping 20cm (8in) off each vine and propagating the prunings in water. Once the roots of each stem are 7cm (3in) in length, create a vertical hole deep enough to place the bottom/rooted half of each cutting into the mother plant's soil, or in a fresh pot to start an entirely new plant. This is what I do to keep my original trailing plant looking full when it becomes a little leggy.

Up the wall

Plants that do well growing on a shelf can also be grown up a wall using self-adhesive hooks from DIY stores. Turn to page 102 to learn more on creating a 'vined living wall'.

A *Hedera helix* has been trained to grow up this wall.

How do I fix crispy leaf tips on a tropical plant?

Before you jump to conclusions thinking your plant is dying, not all brown tips are caused by a 'problem'. As your leaf tirelessly works day and night to photosynthesize and respire, it will eventually show its age by not looking as perfect as humans might expect it to be. Here, I'll teach you some ways to identify and address any issues that are the cause of your leaf abnormalities.

WHAT CAUSES AREAS OF THE LEAF TO DIE?

If there is an absence of new growth emerging from the stems, and the foliage isn't looking its best, there could be an underlying issue either with its environment or within the soil. Situations such as prolonged dehydration, overexposure to the sun, or warm rooms with minimal humidity caused by a nearby operating radiator could be the culprit for premature crisping.

IS MY PLANT DYING?

Although damaged foliage can be a signpost for a dying plant, chances are it's nothing as serious. Start by taking the poorly specimen out of its pot to inspect its subsoil region. Instead of pulling compost from the plant, simply scan the outer edge of the rootball for any signs of root rot (turn to page 166 for symptoms and a remedy).

Areas where the leaf has become brown or crispy will never turn green again. Ensuring your plant receives the correct amount of light, warmth and feed are the first steps to promote a healthier, greener plant.

A large *Dypsis lutescens* sitting majestically in a hallway. Be warned: palms will burn very quickly when nearby radiators are on, so keep this in mind to avoid crispy leaf tips.

Blame evolution

In tropical and temperate forests, where rainfall and humidity are high, rain or dew droplets will trickle to the lowest point of the leaf, which is usually its tip. This area is known as a 'drip tip', and it is where most houseplants become crispy after a few months. Although misting will help increase humidity, creating a 'pebble tray' will provide a more consistent level of airborne moisture around the foliage.

For those that have a healthy root system, check the following points to ensure your tropical houseplant becomes happy again:

- Increase humidity levels by creating a 'pebble tray' for your plant. Fill a plastic or ceramic saucer to the top with stones. Pour water into the saucer, stopping when the water is 2.5cm (1in) below the stones; place the plant on top; keep the reservoir and soil moist.
- Learn to read the soil's moisture levels and water only once the top third dries out or the pot feels lightweight when lifted.
- Keep your houseplants at least 2m (6ft) away from an operating heater but ensure temperatures are above 18°C (64°F).
- Create a monthly fertilizer regime to promote longer-lasting green leaves. A 'houseplant'-labelled feed from a store is perfectly fine. (See page 62 for more info on feeding.)
- Although winter sunlight is beneficial for all houseplants, excessive direct light of more than three hours during the other months should be avoided.
- Check for pests, especially thrips, spider mites and mealybugs. (See pages 132–135 for identification.)

WHAT SHOULD I CUT OFF?

It's now time to get a clean pair of secateurs out.
Indeed, you can use kitchen scissors but just ensure that they are sharp enough for the task. Blunt apparatus can cause further damage to the leaf due to risk of puncturing the surrounding plant tissue. Hold the affected leaf and cut parallel to the crispy tip, slightly into the green region, as shown here.

Will the brown areas come back?

In all cases, a new, thinner band of brown will develop along the new wound – we call this 'callousing' over. This should stop over the next few weeks, but if it continues to spread, remove the entire leaf and admire the healthier growth elsewhere.

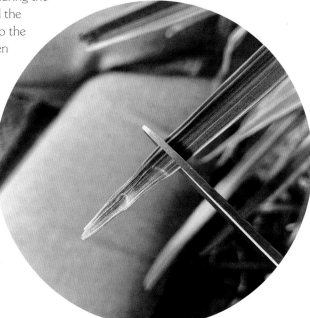

Left: Healthy monstera leaves.

Below: Use scissors to remove crispy brown leaf tips.

I've left my plant outside in the cold for too long – how do I save it?

If your houseplant has developed black or softened leaves, chances are it has been shocked by a cold change of environment. I regularly hear that houseplants can benefit from being placed outside in the summer to 'reset' and push out new growth. While this is true, the risk of leaving a houseplant outside for too long in the cold can indeed cause sudden and lasting problems.

THE SCIENCE BEHIND A COLD-DAMAGED LEAF

Only a handful of houseplants can deal with temperatures below 8°C (46°F) due to evolutionary tolerance back in their natural habitats. Most houseplants are from tropical or warm temperate regions across the continents, and, therefore, are best suited to warm rooms in our homes. When a tropical plant is exposed to unusually cold conditions, its cells can rupture, which limits the overall performance of the stem or leaf. This damage can be localized to just the leaves, but in some cases can be within the stem as well, which poses more of a serious threat to the plant.

Take care when leaving houseplants such as this *Heptapleurum* outside.

COLD-DAMAGE SYMPTOMS

The overall symptoms can vary from plant to plant, but here are a few common signs to look out for:
– A leaf can become 'water-soaked', where it can feel mushy or soft to the touch.
– Black or dark-brown areas across the leaf and stem.
– Severe wilting or leaf drop.
– Leaf edges look burnt.
– Plant becomes loose within the soil when tugged (potentially root rot).

WHAT ARE THE 3 STEPS TO SAVE A COLD PLANT?

1 Relocate the plant to a warmer location, between 16–20°C (61–68°F). Ensure the plant receives enough natural light by placing it on or within 1m (3ft) of a north or east-facing window.

2 Wait 24 hours to water the soil, and when you do, ensure it is lukewarm and not chilled. Moist soil is colder than dry soil, so let's try to avoid chilling the roots out too much!

3 Don't prune the foliage until a week has passed, to fully confirm which leaves have died or become damaged. Prune off any damaged leaves (or whole stems) that have perished. Feel free to take the plant out of its pot to check for root rot, too (turn to page 166 for more information on identifying and addressing this).

Feed with care

For now, try not to over-fertilize your cold-damaged plant. Encouraging it to produce new growth so soon after a traumatic event will divert the energy from a much-needed recovery. It's also good to note that already-damaged plant portions won't 'turn' green again, instead they will remain affected until pruned off.

Five plants that don't mind the cold

As I mention on page 34, most houseplants will survive in temperatures around 15°C (59°F) or above, with only a few being able to go lower. In this section, I'll mention five easy houseplants that will grow in the coldest areas of your home, such as an unheated conservatory or porch.

Pelargoniums

People often grow these plants (sometimes wrongly called geraniums) in gardens due to their long-lasting flowers and fragrant leaves. Ignore the suggestion that you leave these plants outdoors over winter as they'll die, and then have to buy a replacement the following spring. Pelargoniums left on cold windowsills make fantastic winter houseplants and they can go back out in the garden in spring.

Parlour palm (*Chamaedorea elegans*)

This type of palm was popular in the 19th century as it could easily tolerate the cold temperatures in typical middle-class homes of that time. Fast forward to today and they still prove a great choice for this very reason. One note to mention is that they can only survive in temperatures above 10°C (50°F), so avoid these plants if your room goes below this.

Butterwort (*Pinguicula*)

Not only are *Pinguiculas* not overly fussy with care requirements, they make great fly-catchers; fungus gnats and mosquitos tend to be their most common food. They'll grow well in any sunny windowsill that has temperatures above 8°C (46°F).

Christmas cactus (*Schlumbergera × buckleyi*)

The trusty Christmas cactus is a great choice for those who have a cold porch or unheated conservatory. As long as the temperatures don't dip below 8°C (46°F), you'll welcome this easy, non-fussy plant into your home. Just don't water the soil during cold spells to avoid the roots rotting from the cold air and compost moisture.

False castor oil plant (*Fatsia japonica*)

Certainly the leafiest plant on this list, the fatsia is a plant that is often grown in gardens. Not many know that this plant also serves well as a houseplant when given enough light. If your porch or conservatory receives bright light (some sun is great), then this plant is for you.

Five more plants

- Jade tree (*Crassula ovata*)
- Cyclamen
- Spider plant (*Chlorophytum comosum*)
- Mistletoe cacti (*Rhipsalis baccifera*)
- Clivia

Why does my plant lose its leaves when it is dormant?

Some specimens, such as amaryllis, cyclamen and oxalis, enter a dormancy period when most, or all, of their leaves die back. In some cases this period may occur in the height of summer, so it is not exclusively in the winter months.

LOOKING AFTER DORMANT PLANTS

Here are some steps you can take to look after your plants when they are dormant:

A close-up shot of *Oxalis triangularis* showcases its deep purple foliage and pale-pink flowers.

1 You will know when your plant is preparing for a period of rest as its growth will halt and the mature leaves will begin to yellow and brown. Once this occurs, you have the choice to allow the plant to decline further, or simply cut off all of its foliage (healthy leaves, too) to put a stop to its growing season.

2 Keep the plant in the soil (and pot) and relocate it to a cool, bright windowsill. Partial sunlight is perfect as this will offer a little warmth. Provide infrequent waters by hydrating the potting mix every few weeks, allowing it to almost dry out in between drinks.

3 After three months (or whenever the plant begins to regrow), relocate the plant into a warmer part of your home and increase watering slightly. (There is no right or wrong to how much, just don't drench the soil too often.) Remember to use a 'houseplant'-labelled feed every third water, too. You should begin to notice shoots appear from the soil or plant, which is a sign that the dormancy period is over.

4 If your plant does not wake up after six months, check the roots for any signs of root rot and act accordingly (see page 166).

Do my plants need special treatment?

Having a collection of several hundred plants, I have learned that there are four main plant groups within the world of houseplant care. These mostly differ in watering and light needs, but within each group, some skills and techniques can be used on any plant.

Bottom left: A *Dionaea muscipula* showing the plant's digestive areas.

Bottom right: Five different cacti.

Top right: A perfect example of a *Nephrolepis*.

CARNIVOROUS PLANTS

Specialist knowledge is needed to successfully grow insect-loving species such as Venus flytraps (*Dionaea muscipula*), trumpet pitchers (*Sarracenia*) and monkey cups (*Nepenthes*). Try to only use rainwater. If this isn't available, use either distilled water, or boiled and cooled tap water. Never feed with fertilizer: the chemicals and minerals will kill your plant. Instead, place your specimen outside (or near a window) during the summer months, in a shaded area, to catch their own prey; you will be surprised how well they attract insects! Provide continual moist soil, or sit the pot in a pool of water (no more than a quarter of the pot's height). Dehydration kills, so don't forget them!

It's okay if some of the leaves/traps yellow and die. Carnivorous plants should go through a dormancy period, so if this is occurring with yours, be sure to keep it in the coolest windowsill possible until new growth emerges. Keep the soil moist throughout this resting period.

They rarely need repotting but if you do choose to repot your plant (or place it in a cool insect-eating terrarium, which I recommend), make sure you only use 'carnivorous'-labelled soil. Never use any other soil medium as the fertilizers and minerals may damage the roots.

FERNS

People often think that ferns grow exclusively in shady parts of the home. However, I have found this not to be the case on several occasions. I grow six different species or varieties at home, all benefiting from a bright, nearby grow light, or a north-east-facing windowsill that offers a smidge of morning sunlight (until 9am). I have found that ferns grown in areas more than 2m (6ft) away from a window will quickly develop yellowing leaves and have a slower rate of new growth compared to those kept in adequate lighting.

CACTI AND SUCCULENTS

For information on watering requirements for this group of plants, see page 42. Essentially, it's all about allowing the soil to fully dry out in between drinks, so that your cactus or succulent has enough time to rest and use up the moisture from the previous drink. Always provide an area with partial sunlight during the day. This means that an east, south or west-facing windowsill is best, as it will provide a couple hours of much-needed rays either in the morning, afternoon or evening, respectively. If, however, you only have a north-facing window available, this will still be fine, but you must allow the soil to remain dry for over a month in between drinks, as the plant's growth rate will be lower.

ORCHIDS

This group is special for several reasons. Firstly, orchids really benefit from their foliage being misted with a solution of water and an 'orchid'-labelled feed. Some growers focus more on feeding their plants via a mist instead of applying it to the soil.

Secondly, their roots can change colour depending on their moisture needs and overall health. Grey/silver roots tell us that the plant needs a drink; whereas if the roots are green it means the specimen is sufficiently hydrated.

The third and final colour is brown, which means the individual strand is dead. Two or three dead roots are fine, but if you can count more than three, take the plant out of its pot to perform a transplant: prune any affected roots back to the base of the stem using a clean pair of scissors.

If less than half of the roots have rotted away, repot using the next-sized transparent pot and a brand of orchid bark. Place a 4cm (1½in) layer of fresh bark in the new pot before resting the roots on top. Fill the remaining gaps with more bark until the pot is four-fifths full.

If less than half of the roots are healthy, be sure to clean and reuse the original pot and repot using orchid bark. Similarly to transplanting a healthy root system, place a 2.5cm (1in) layer of fresh bark into the pot before resting the roots on top. Fill any remaining gaps with more bark until the pot is three-quarters full.

PESTS THAT MAY ATTACK ORCHIDS

Generally speaking, orchids are pest-free, as most critters stay away from them. Their thick leaves and lack of soil make it more difficult for smaller pests such as aphids and spider mites to bite into the leaves. The only pest that can do some damage are mealybugs. Keep an eye out for them around orchid flowers and leaves, where small cubbyholes can house an infestation. Typical symptoms are white, cotton-like 'fluffs' that'll be slightly sticky, as well as the bug itself. See page 164 to learn more on mealybug eradication. Another pest to look out for are fungus gnats, but these won't damage the overall plant, so that's a relief. The only time that these will become present is when you'll water the bark too often. Remember – you only need to rehydrate the plant once its roots turn silver in the pot!

Orchids in the sun

Moth orchids can be suited to a windowsill with partial sunlight, so why not try keeping them on a north-east or north-west-facing window? I've found that a small amount of direct light per day does a great deal for longer flowering times and overall better health.

The pink and white flowers of *Phalaenopsis* 'Nemesis'.

How should I transport my plants?

For those of us who frequently move house or possessions (due to being at university, for example), transporting plants can be difficult. Not only are the logistics rather challenging, but also the risk of a leaf or stem being snapped can put many people off attempting it in the first place. Unfortunately, I was one of those people who suffered a few broken plants along the way, but I'm here to share some of my best tips for avoiding heartbreak at the end of the journey.

PREPARING A HOUSEPLANT FOR A JOURNEY

1   Water the soil well a few hours beforehand. Not only will this help the soil stay in its pot during transit, but it will also downplay the risk of dehydration caused by sunlight and air circulation (when the windows are open).

2   There's no need to repot before moving. A loose rootball is more likely to rattle around and come out of its pot, making a right mess in your car!

3   When packing your vehicle with plants, it's good to know that most plants' stems and leaves have more flexibility being tied so they are positioned upwards against the stem. Try to allow the stems' tips, however, to be bent downwards (towards the soil) as this will significantly decrease the risk of them being snapped off.

NIFTY TIPS

- For tall plants, make sure you put them into·the car pot-first. This will limit the risk of stems and leaves snapping, as they would do more easily if placed foliage-first through the door. You can also keep these plants sideways in a car as long as they are secure and don't obstruct the driver's field of vision.

- Medium-sized plants (below 1m/3ft in height) can be placed upright on the ground directly behind the front seats. When placed on the floor, ensure the leaves or stems don't get bent downwards if pushing the front seat backwards to pin the pot between the seats.

- Place small plants in a transparent box (after a quick check for pests) and ensure the pots don't budge an inch. If there are a few gaps for the plants to accidentally slide into when you're driving, place socks in between the pots.

- Sit smaller plants in empty shoes, or wedge them in the corner of the boot with bags or clothes.

Take care when moving your plants. Here a *Spathiphyllum wallisii*, *Chlorophytum comosum*, ficus and *Chamaedorea elegans* have been safely arranged in the boot of a car.

Keep them warm

If you're travelling in winter, don't get caught out by cold temperatures overnight! Keep plants indoors until your journey commences in the morning. You can, however, leave any houseplants in the car overnight as long as the outdoor temperature is above 16°C (61°F).

What happens to my plants when I go away on holiday?

Coming from someone who has hundreds of houseplants, trying to have a holiday can be tricky. In this section, I'll enlighten you with a few tips I've learnt to delay the soil-drying process, so you don't need to worry about coming home to dehydrated plants.

3 CONDITIONS THAT WILL DEHYDRATE YOUR PLANT

1. **Sunlight**: The brighter the light, the quicker the compost will dry, especially in direct sun.

2. **Warmth**: Temperatures above 18°C (64°F) will increase photosynthesis and transpiration (moisture loss in the plant's leaves), along with quickening evaporation in the soil. This includes keeping a plant within 2m (6ft) of an operating radiator.

3. **Water**: It sounds basic, but an unwatered plant will quickly turn into a dehydrated one.

3 STEPS TO KEEP YOUR PLANTS HYDRATED WHILE YOU'RE ON HOLIDAY

1 Ensure each plant has had a thorough drink before you leave. Soak the soil until water starts dripping from the drainage hole(s) below, and discard the excess moisture. Aim to use lukewarm water to avoid shocking the plant.

2 Create a couple of pebble trays (see page 167). If you don't have a pebble tray, simply fill three jugs or containers with 1L (2 pints) of water. In a group, sit the plants on each pebble tray on the floor around 1.3m (4ft) from a windowsill. Keep them tight together, but just far enough apart so their leaves don't touch, in case of pests. Being on the floor will be cooler than being on a table or windowsill, so the plants won't need to work as hard to fight the warmth. The water from the tray or jugs will evaporate and increase the humidity around the plants.

3 Or, place your plants in a transparent tub or box. The higher humidity levels in the box will almost stop moisture loss in its tracks and is the best way to avoid death by dehydration. Drill a few holes in the lid, or leave it slightly ajar, to allow the air to circulate. Just remember to keep the box of plants in a windowsill so they can receive enough light.

A collection of cacti: golden barrel cactus, *Lobivia ancistrophora*, *Mammillaria* and *Disocactus flagelliformis*.

Holiday priorities

The number one rule for holiday plant care is to remember the three dehydrating factors: high temperatures (above 24°C/75°F), excessive sunlight on the foliage, and/or being pot-bound. With the latter, try repotting your houseplant a week before going away.

Can I care for my houseplants sustainably?

Do you ever worry about how your love of houseplants might be affecting the planet? Between 2017 and 2019, the houseplant industry increased 50 per cent in sales year-on-year, which then doubled again during the pandemic. While bringing nature indoors has been proven to be highly beneficial for us, the industry is still learning how to improve its sustainability for the sake of our planet.

Sustainable soil 'ingredient' alternatives

Some soil aggregates (ingredients) are better than others in terms of the ecological effects they have when being manufactured. For example, perlite is made from volcanic glass and in its production, it needs to be heated up to at least 700°C (1,292°F), which consumes a great level of energy. Perlite is a non-renewable resource and the mining of it disturbs local habitats, too. By choosing the alternatives below, you're contributing to a more environmentally friendly industry and hobby.

Soil additive (used to improve the soil)	Why is it used?	A better alternative?
Perlite	For aeration and to avoid soil compaction	Rice hulls or pumice
Grit	Improves soil structure and aids drainage	Crushed seashells, sold online as a by-product of the seafood industry. Not vegan.
Vermiculite	Moisture retention	Fine-grade biochar, which uses otherwise-discarded wood and is carbon negative
Bark	Moisture retention and improves soil structure	Biochar; some use larger grade for better soil structure

Use old soil elsewhere

After repotting a plant or discarding one that has died, you may wonder what to do with the leftover soil. I would recommend mulching it into the garden's top soil layer or placing it in a compost bin to bulk up contents for maturity. I would, however, advise against using this soil for another houseplant if the original died of root rot, to prevent the spread of disease.

Shop local

You may have come across the term 'food miles', where ingredients have travelled from overseas to be sold in another country. Well, the horticultural equivalent of this is 'plant miles', with some species being shipped as far as Southeast Asia. Although finding alternative, local sellers of the same plant can be a struggle, there are many swap events in which both amateur and professional sellers exchange plants and/or seeds.

Reuse water

The best way to hydrate a plant is by pouring enough water into the soil until it drains out of the bottom of the pot. Especially when you've mixed in fertilizer, this excess moisture can be re-poured into a neighbouring plant to reduce water wastage.

Reuse plastic pots

According to reports, only 10 per cent of local authorities accept plastic pots for recycling. Two ways in which we can help reduce wasted pots is by reusing old ones from previous plants (clean them before each reuse to avoid disease spread), or buy alternatives such as coconut coir. And when it is time to say 'goodbye' to that plastic pot, take it to a garden centre or DIY store that hosts a recycling scheme. This applies to empty compost bags, too.

Hold on to your dying plants

Chances are, there is life in your old plant yet. People are often scared that a plant with only a few leaves will never recover. In fact, the plant has a back-up mechanism that should kick-start a revival, if you know what to do. See pages 164–169 for common plant problems and remedies.

Is my plant poorly?

Most plant owners panic when they see a less-than-perfect leaf, but this is part of nature. Each one will wither to make space for a new one. The yellowing/browning process allows the plant to divert minerals to an area that where they're needed more, such as powering a new leaf. However, it may be the sign of something more serious, in which case refer to this list of the most common symptoms and their causes.

Issue	What it Looks Like	Symptom
Sun-scorch		Burnt leaves due to overexposure to the sun that feel dry or crispy to the touch. Often accompanied by curling/wilting foliage.
Mealybugs		White cottony/fluffy patches will develop on the leaves, flowers and stems. Leaves can become brown/brown-yellow. Pest appearance: Similar to a grain of sand.
Spider mites		Small, yellow dots will appear on the leaf, along with silvery webs that house the mites' eggs. Pest appearance: White and ovular, with small scales and legs.

Remedy & Useful Advice

Your plant has become used to a bright setting. Don't relocate it to a dark area of the home as this will cause environmental shock. Relocate it to a windowsill that gets minimal-to-no direct sunlight.

Never keep a pest-ridden plant within 30cm (12in) of an unaffected specimen. If possible, keep it in another room to minimize spread. Wipe the foliage with a soapy damp cloth before hosing it, then finely mist both sides of the leaves with a pesticide.

Never keep a pest-ridden plant within 30cm (12in) of an unaffected specimen. If possible, keep it in another room to minimize spread. Wipe the foliage down with a soapy damp cloth before hosing (in the sink, shower or outdoors). Use a specialist plant-based control spray by finely misting both sides of the leaves.

Issue	What it Looks Like	Symptom
Thrips		Rapid yellowing and browning of leaves within days. Small, brown, raised spots may develop in the yellowed leaf regions, too. Pest appearance: Yellow, oblong bodies 1–2mm (0.4–0.8in) in length. Adults will be black and a similar size.
Aphids and blackfly		Green or black bugs will appear on the juvenile growth of a plant. Each pest can grow to 2–4mm (0.08–0.2in) in length when mature.
Fungus gnats		Small, black flies that hover around the soil and can lay over 150 eggs in their lifetime.
Low humidity		Brown leaf tips and a shortened lifespan of any present flowers.
Root rot or transplant shock		Wilting, leaf curling and yellowing/ browning foliage

Remedy

Don't ignore the pests. Thrips are airborne, so they'll spread to other houseplants within a few weeks. The most common groups of plants to be affected are palms, aroids (monsteras, peace lilies, devil's ivy), dracaenas, yucca and bird-of-paradise. Take immediate action, along with checking all other houseplants in your collection (except cacti and succulents, which aren't usually affected). Wipe the foliage down with a soapy damp cloth before hosing (in the sink, shower or outdoors). Use a specialist control spray to mist both sides of the leaves.

Don't ignore these pests. Although their damage is often limited due to their weak mouths, it's critical to address the infestation at first sight. Squish each bug with your hands or use a warm soapy cloth. Most pesticides will work, but you can also make a homemade solution by boiling a garlic clove for 10 minutes in water, before spraying it on the foliage once cooled.

Don't panic. This pest is entirely harmless to the plant and us, so take your time! Replace the top third of the potting mix with a fresh batch of 'houseplant'-labelled soil. This will remove the eggs and stop another gnat cycle in its tracks. Always replace the soil for each houseplant, not just a couple. In some cases, the presence of gnats means the soil is being kept too moist. Allow the compost to dry out for a little longer in between waterings, if possible.

Don't panic about leaves that don't look perfect. Most of the time, browning leaf tips are the by-product of maturity, whereby the leaf is just showing its age. Keep plants at least 2m (6ft) away from operating radiators, unless they are cacti or succulents. Create a 'pebble tray', whereby you get a tray and fill it to the very top with stones, before pouring water into the tray (and stones), until the water line is slightly below the tops of the stones. The plant must sit on top of the stones and not be submerged in the water, as a pebble tray is to only evaporate moisture around the foliage and not to provide soil moisture.

Keep the plant well-fed and make sure it is kept in suitable light levels. If you're struggling for an ideal location in the home, try a sunless windowsill. For suspicion of root rot, take the plant out of its pot and check the colour of the roots. Healthy roots will be light-coloured and plump, whereas dying roots will be brown, squishy and can be easily pulled-off from the plant. While holding the plant's stem, gently rinse off the soil from the roots and gently shake the rootball. Prune off the dead roots with sharp scissors and repot in a pot that's only 3–5cm (1–2in) smaller than its original one. For cases where there are zero healthy roots remaining, take stem cuttings as mentioned on page 85.
Cont.

Issue	What it Looks Like	Symptom
Leaf spot diseases		Small, yellow or brown dots/circles on foliage. Could be caused by fungal spores, a viral infection or bacteria.
Small new leaves (compared to the older ones)		Leaves that are significantly smaller than the plant's original ones when purchased, due to the change in environmental conditions.
A lack of new growth (leaves)		Unless the plant's current leaves are becoming unhealthy (yellow, brown or are dropping off), the plant should be fine. If, however, the plant isn't growing and is looking a little scrappy, read page 166 about root rot. If you're considering relocating your plant, make sure it doesn't receive sunlight if it's not used to it. Don't place it within 2m (6ft) of operating radiator either; as long as the room is naturally warm your plant will be happy..
Continual leaf drop		Leaves may develop small, dark markings on the foliage before dropping off quickly. It can be caused by pests or lack of light.

Remedy

For suspicion of transplant shock, create a pebble tray (mentioned in 'Low Humidity' on page 167), and mist the foliage once every two days. If the plant is still wilting after two weeks, don't be tempted to water the soil too frequently. Allow the top third of the soil to dry in between hydrations and always use lukewarm water to avoid shocking the plant further. If the plant continues to wilt after six weeks, take stem cuttings as mentioned on page 85.

Never forget to wash any used apparatus after addressing a potential disease. Failure to do so may lead to the infection being unintentionally spread to other plants. Remedies can be tricky as there are no cures for affected areas of the plant. Prune the affected leaves and change the soil, too, for a fresh batch of an indoor potting mix. (Coconut coir potting mixes are a good choice.) Keep the plant well-fed and ensure it's kept in a bright location with minimal sunlight – a north-east or north-west-facing windowsill is best.

Don't panic. As long as the plant is growing and holding its leaves green, even if it takes a few years, it will grow larger leaves. Enjoy the journey and not the destination!
Ensure the plant receives the right amount of light (see Right Place, Right Plant chapter) and maintain a good fertilization regime (see Feeding, Repotting and Making New Plants chapter).
Some sources recommend repotting a plant if it's pot-bound, but I don't find this to be the end-all remedy. If the plant is growing happily in its current pot, don't transplant.

Unless the leaves are unhealthy, the plant should be fine. If the plant isn't growing and is looking a little scrappy, check for root rot (see page 166). If you're considering relocating your plant, make sure it doesn't receive sunlight if it's not used to it. Don't place it within 2m (6ft) of an operating radiator – if the room is warm your plant will be happy. Like us, plants deserve a rest from time to time. Some plants will take a longer dormancy period than others, but if you're worried about a lack of growth, have a go at these:

• Relocate to a warmer or brighter area to stimulate new growth.
• Increase fertilization. Even during the autumn and winter months, it's important to feed tropical plants as the limited daylight hours won't help.

Don't put the plant in direct sunlight. Check for pests (see pages 132–135) as the plant may be responding by removing some of its most affected leaves. Try increasing light levels.

Issue	What it Looks Like	Symptom
Loss of flowers		A sudden loss of flowers since purchasing; flowers suddenly drying up and dropping off; or a total lack of new flowers developing.
Leaf drop on plants that have periods of dormancy		Most (if not all) of the leaves fall off, but most come back in the following season.

Remedy

Don't worry about a gradual loss of flowers on orchids and peace lilies, as it is entirely normal for them. If you haven't had any blooms for over a year, don't repot! A pot-bound root system is more likely to cause flowers as the restricted space will trick the plant into thinking it's dying. This sounds harsh but the plant will be okay. In many cases, the plant is only flowering to reproduce and kick-start the next generation of flowers, so this stress will only entice a more probable show of blooms.

If all the flowers have begun to wilt and drop off, this could be a sign of dehydration, artificial heat (from a radiator), or environmental shock when it was brought home from the store. Ensure the plant is fed regularly (every third water using a 'houseplant'-labelled feed) and in a bright but sunless windowsill.

If you've waited over a year for a show of bloom, try the following:

- For orchids and amaryllis, increase sunlight levels.
- Bring the plant closer to the window or place it in a north-east or south-west-facing window so that it receives up to two hours of sunlight per day. Short periods of sunlight per day may increase the likelihood of new flowers being developed.
- Avoid sunlight for plants such as peace lilies, though, as they prefer a sheltered spot around 1m (3ft) away from a window.
- Keep watering to a minimum to force stress onto the plant. Allow an orchid's roots to turn silver before giving it a water – check this by glancing through its transparent pot. The plant is sufficiently hydrated while the roots are green in colour. For amaryllis, allow all of the soil to dry out for around 7–10 days before giving it another drink. Tropical plants need to be kept a little more moist, so ensure they don't wilt too often in between drinks. Feed often with a 'houseplant'-labelled feed and apply this to the water for every third drink.

Don't water the soil too frequently while there are no leaves. Keep the soil relatively dry during the plant's dormancy period. See page 42 for more information .

Index

Acknowledgements & Credits

ACKNOWLEDGEMENTS

I'd like to give a special 'thank you' to Sorrel, Dominique & Julie for assisting me with my first book – and my Dad, who took over my business' orders whilst I focused on writing!

PICTURE CREDITS

Adobe Stock/FollowTheFlow: 62-63. **Alamy**/Daniel Borzynski: 10 (top left); Valtteri Laine: 102; Sanja: 154. Joe Bagley: 147. **Biodiversity Heritage Library**/Missouri Botanical Garden: 9. **Dreamstime**/Saletomic: 160-161. **Getty Images**/Beekeepx: 159; Byakkaya: 137; Delmaine Donson: 94-95, 108 (bottom); Fotostorm: 149; FreshSplash: 44, 52; Kenneth Keifer/500px: 10 (bottom left). **iStock**/Dewin'Indew: 105; Anastasia Dobrusina: 119; Elisa Festa: 59 (top left); Andrii Horulko: 123; Malija: 12 (left); Qnula: 122 (left). **Living4Media**/Karl Anderson: 121; Christine Bauer: 89; Britta Bloggt: 99; Monique Ton Bouwer: 98 (bottom); Anne den Haan: 79 (top); Barbara Hibler: 47; Marij Hessel: 91; Hsfoto: 80; Camilla Isaksson: 23; Bjarni B. Jacobsen: 97; Cecilia Möller: 24 (bottom left), 65, 142. **www.maddieanneinteriors.co.uk**: 116 (top). **Nature Picture Library**/Nick Garbutt: 10 (top right). **Pexels**/Cottonbro: 73 (top), 73 (bottom); Teona Swift: 36-37, 40, 51 (top), 83. **Shutterstock**/AjayTvm: 66 (bottom left); Amberkory: 153; AS-photo: 66 (top right); Asy Asy: 168 (2nd from bottom); BoxBoy: 164 (top); Chekyravaa: 113; Julia Cherk: 170 (top), 170 (bottom); ChWeiss: 168 (top); CoinUp: 51 (bottom right); DimaBerlin: 116 (bottom left); Eugene_Photo: 67 (centre); Followtheflow: 14-15, 108 (top left); Nor Gal: 66 (top left); Dasha Gerasimova: 139; Wat Hiran: 12 (right); Wilfred Huddlestone: 66 (bottom centre); IMG Stock Studio: 129; Isabel Eve: 29 (bottom); Kckate16: 164 (centre); Tomasz Klejdysz: 166 (top), 166 (bottom); LightField Studios: 128; Liloon: 98 (top); Maritxu: 140-141; Amelia Martin: 166 (centre); Jacqui Martin: 13 (left); Martino77: 24 (bottom right); MT.Photostock: 155 (top); Anastasiia Murko: 51 (bottom left); New Africa: 60-61, 70, 124,155 (bottom); Nice-pics-125: 166 (2nd from bottom); Nuttapong: 67 (bottom); Chansom Pantip: 165; Qnula: 122 (right), 127; RPA Studio: 66 (top centre), 66 (bottom right); Semiglass: 168 (bottom); Nadya So: 29 (top); Bogdan Sonjachnyj: 68; Vinicius R. Souza: 166 (2nd from top); TippyTortue: 115; Tunatura: 164 (bottom); Vikram W: 168 (2nd from top); Yurii_Yarema: 59 (bottom left); Yuryevna39: 157. **Soil.Ninja**: 67 (top). **Photography by Jacqui Turk. Design and styling by Jono Fleming**: 104. **Unsplash**/Evangeline Bautista: 59 (top right), 59 (bottom right); Brina Blum: 107; Ekaterina Bolychevtseva: 79 (bottom left); David Clode: 10 (bottom right); Curology: 57; Yehleen Gaffney: 30-31; Angele Kamp: 116; Chris Lee: 7; Jeremy Lee: 146; Virginia Marinova: 84; Magali Merzougui: 24 (top), 79 (bottom right); Corey O'Connell: 108 (top right); Annie Spratt: 55; Milada Vigerova: 112. **Visions**/Bakker: 13 (right).